DIVOF

THE THINGS YOU THOUGHT
YOU'D NEVER NEED TO KNOW

DIVORCE

THE THINGS YOU THOUGHT YOU'D NEVER NEED TO KNOW

JILL M BLACK QC
and ELIZABETH R AUCKLAND

RIGHT WAY

CONTENTS

NOTE: This book deals with the law in force in England and Wales only. Whilst the legal position in relation to divorces in Scotland and Northern Ireland may be similar to that described here in many respects, there are also important differences.

If your divorce will be dealt with in Scotland or Northern Ireland, you are advised to refer to a publication that deals specifically with the law of the country concerned, or to consult a solicitor in the appropriate country.

PART 1:
GENERAL INFORMATION AND
FIRST CONSIDERATIONS

1
About this Book

No one gets married expecting their marriage to end in divorce and you may have thought of divorce as someone else's problem – something that will never happen to you. Most people are prepared to offer sympathy and advice to friends and relations who are going through the process of separation and divorce. But, if your marriage starts to break down, it comes as a shock and as you embark on the business of getting divorced you may feel anxious, helpless and very lonely. To be faced at such a time with unfamiliar and sometimes complicated legal procedures can be very daunting.

Most people appreciate the assistance of a solicitor at all stages of their divorce, and for some matters you really cannot do without the advice of a solicitor. This book is designed primarily for those who are consulting a solicitor but who would like to read about what is involved in the process of getting divorced and how it is likely to affect them. It does not therefore give you instructions for a do-it-yourself divorce. If you are contemplating dealing with everything yourself, you should still find this book interesting and instructive reading but you will need to refer to other publications for further details of the procedure involved.

Getting divorced almost always involves a great deal more than simply obtaining the decree of the court that ends your marriage. You will have to cope with all sorts of problems over your property, about the children, over money, etc. This book will give you an overall picture of the way in which the divorce itself is obtained and of how the more usual other problems that arise when a family breaks up are resolved. The more you understand about what is happening, the more confident you should feel about the situation. Not only will you be able to make your solicitor's job easier because you will have a good idea of the sort of information that he requires from you but you will also be sure that you are not missing out on help from your solicitor or the courts, simply because you did not know that it was available.

Divorce law has grown up slowly through legislation made by Parliament and through cases decided by the courts. A lot of the law is complex and detailed and it would be impossible to go into it all in a book this size. One of the problems of a book on divorce is that divorce is never the same for any two families because, of course, each family has its own individual problems. Nevertheless, the basic legal procedures do not differ from case to case and a lot of the difficulties associated with a divorce crop up time and again. This book does not attempt to cover unusual points that may arise in a few divorces nor can it give personal advice to each reader. It simply aims to help you cope with most of the problems that you will encounter in the course of your divorce and to provide you with a basic knowledge of the law as it is likely to affect you.

Changes in the law in recent years

New legislation and changes in family policy are introduced all the time and you will probably have heard of some of the more high profile developments.

The Pensions Act 1995, for example, changed the law on many aspects of pensions including the way in which courts can deal with pension arrangements for divorcing couples. Since July 1996 a spouse who has inadequate pension provision has been able to get a court order giving him or her a share of the other spouse's pension on retirement, in some circumstances. A further reform which came into effect in 2000 now allows the court to divide the pension on divorce so that each spouse has a share of it to invest. Chapter 20 includes more detail about this in the section about pensions.

Another piece of legislation which received considerable press coverage was the Family Law Act 1996. Although the Family Law Act was passed by parliament under the previous government in 1996, some parts of the Act have never taken effect. The proposed changes in procedure for getting a divorce which would have introduced what was known as 'no fault divorce' were not popular and the government has decided not to go ahead with them. On the other hand, the current law on personal protection and occupation of the family home (details of which you will find in Chapter 12) and mediation (Chapter 17) was introduced by the Family Law Act.

Another change in recent years has been the replacement of the Legal Aid Board by the Legal Services Commission in April 2000. You will find information regarding the current position on what is now known as 'public funding' (rather than 'legal aid') in Chapter 4 and there are numerous references to public funding throughout the book.

The current law relating to issues arising about children of divorcing parents has been in force since the implementation of the Children Act 1989. However, there have been more recent reforms affecting the roles of the people who prepare reports about children for the courts: in 2001 a new body called the Children and Family Court Advisory and Support Service (CAFCASS) came into being, which coordinates the roles of court welfare officers and guardians ad litem. You will find references to 'children and family court reporters', whose role was created with the introduction of CAFCASS, in Part 4 of this book.

The Child Support Act 1991 brought into existence the Child Support Agency (CSA) which was intended to set the level of child maintenance for all children of separated parents. However, the formula used to calculate maintenance was extremely complex so applications to the CSA were often subject to delay and errors: in March 2003 reforms were introduced simplifying the maintenance calculations. You will find more information about this in Chapter 20.

How this book is organised

As you will see from the contents page, the book is divided into seven parts, including specific sections on the children (Part 4) and financial arrangements (Part 6), topics common to most divorces. Part 5 includes a chapter about mediation. Although divorce nearly always brings with it feelings of anger and bitterness, everyone in your family will gain both emotionally and financially if you and your spouse are able to deal with the problems arising because of your separation and divorce with the minimum acrimony. Since the introduction of publicly funded mediation, the opportunity has been there for divorcing couples to deal with issues in a more amicable way, and a glance at this chapter is recommended for most people reading this book.

The book also covers the divorce procedure itself (Part 2) and a section about domestic violence and harassment (Part 3). The final chapter contains details of some relevant organisations and publications which may be helpful if you are considering or going through a divorce.

2

An Introduction to Divorce

As far as possible this book steers clear of technical legal terms. Nevertheless, getting divorced is a legal procedure and you are bound to hear lawyers and court officials using unfamiliar terms. Where technical terms are used in this book, you will generally find them explained when they are first mentioned. However, there are several words that you need to understand at the outset. The purpose of this chapter is to explain them and to give you a bird's eye view of the whole process of getting a divorce – once you have absorbed these basic terms there should be no difficulty in understanding the rest of the book.

The bare bones of the divorce procedure
The formal procedure for obtaining a divorce begins when one spouse decides that the marriage is at an end and presents the divorce court with a formal document known as the *divorce petition* asking for the marriage to be terminated. This book has generally been written on the basis that it is the wife who will be seeking the divorce – this is for the sake of simplicity only and the choice of the wife rather than the husband is entirely arbitrary. In fact, both husband and wife have exactly the same rights to seek a divorce and you can take it that anything which is said in relation to a wife in the following chapters will also apply to the husband and vice versa, unless the contrary is expressly stated.

Once the divorce procedure is under way, the spouse who presented the petition will be known as the *petitioner* and the other spouse will be known as the *respondent*.

A step by step outline of the course of divorce proceedings follows below. The proceedings do not actually affect the marriage in any way until the court pronounces a *decree nisi* of divorce. This is a provisional court order indicating that, provided there are no unforeseen hitches (such as problems over the arrangements that have been made for the children) the court will be prepared to grant a final divorce in a few weeks. The divorce becomes permanent and fully effective only when this final order is made – it is called the *decree absolute* of divorce. Not until this stage is reached is either spouse free to remarry.

When one spouse seeks a divorce because of adultery of the other spouse, and names the other person involved in the adultery in the divorce petition, that person is entitled to have his or her say in the divorce proceedings and is known as the *co-respondent*.

The procedure step by step

1. The petitioner consults a solicitor about divorce (or, if she intends to deal with the divorce herself, goes to the county court office to obtain the necessary forms and explanatory leaflets about divorce procedure).

2. The divorce papers are prepared (for example, the divorce petition and a statement as to the arrangements that are being made for the children after the divorce).

3. The divorce papers are 'filed' (or formally presented) at the court office by the petitioner or her solicitor. The divorce proceedings are now under way.

4. If either spouse is in immediate financial difficulty, he or she can ask the court to make a temporary maintenance order for him or herself.

5. The court sends the respondent (and the co-respondent if there is one) copies of the divorce papers and instructions on what he should do about the divorce.

6. The respondent (and co-respondent) decide(s) whether he wants to seek advice from a solicitor and consults one, at once, if he decides he does.

7. The respondent (and co-respondent) decide(s) whether he wishes to object to the divorce being granted.

8. The respondent (and co-respondent) or his solicitor complete(s) the form known as the acknowledgement of service which he will have received from the court with the divorce papers, showing that he has received all the documents and indicating what he proposes to do about the divorce. He should do this within seven days of receiving the papers in the first place.

9. In most cases the respondent (and co-respondent) will indicate that they do not wish to oppose the divorce. The court will then notify the petitioner that she can proceed with the case.

10. The petitioner or her solicitor completes a form known as an affidavit of evidence, confirming that what she said in her petition is correct. She will be required to swear on the Bible or affirm that this is so in the presence of another solicitor.

11. The petitioner or her solicitor delivers the affidavit to the court office and asks the court to give directions about the granting of the divorce decree.

12. The district judge considers the case privately. If he is satisfied that the petitioner is entitled to a divorce, he fixes the day on which this will be pronounced by the court.

13. The court informs the petitioner and the respondent (and the co-respondent) when the divorce decree will be pronounced.

14. The judge or the district judge pronounces decree nisi of divorce in court. Either party can attend if they wish, but neither is normally obliged to do so.

15. The court is now able to consider long term financial arrangements – when it actually does so will depend on all the circumstances of the particular case.

16. Provided that there are no problems over the arrangements for the children, the petitioner has only to wait for six weeks to elapse from the date on which decree nisi was pronounced before she can apply for the final divorce decree, decree absolute. This application will be made by her or her solicitor at the court office.

17. Decree absolute is granted. The court sends a certificate of decree absolute to the petitioner and the respondent. The divorce is now complete and both spouses are now free to remarry. There may, however, be outstanding questions relating to the children, or over property or maintenance. These will be cleared up as soon as possible.

You will notice that no mention has been made of the earliest time when you can ask the court to decide issues over the children (for example where they are going to live and what contact the absent parent is going to have) or to step in to help where one of the spouses or the children need personal protection from the other spouse. This is because with such serious matters it is always possible to obtain help from the court, if necessary, even before divorce proceedings have been commenced.

Judicial separation and nullity

You may have heard of two other court orders that can affect a marriage – a decree of *nullity* and a decree of *judicial separation*. Neither of these is very common these days.

A decree of nullity is used to terminate a marriage instead of a decree of divorce when for some reason the marriage has never been properly valid. This can happen if, for example, the marriage has never been consummated by sexual intercourse because one spouse has refused to have sexual intercourse or has been unable to do so or where the marriage was never a proper marriage because the spouses were too closely related to each other. Once a degree of nullity has been pronounced, both parties are free to remarry just as they are after a divorce.

If it turns out that a nullity decree would be more appropriate than a divorce in your case, your solicitor will tell you and will see that all the necessary steps are taken for you. Although the procedure will be similar in some respects to the procedure for getting a divorce, there will be differences, for example, you will have to attend a court hearing when the judge will determine whether you should be granted a decree of nullity or not. The court will be able to resolve questions of finance and property, difficulties over the children, etc., just as it can when it grants a divorce.

A decree of judicial separation does not actually end the marriage and neither spouse is free to remarry after it. What it does do is to give the court's formal seal of approval to the spouses' living apart. The court can resolve all the problems that are likely to attend the separation (over property, children, etc.) just as it can when it grants a divorce. The procedure for obtaining a judicial separation is almost identical to that for obtaining a divorce, except that there is only one decree of judicial separation whereas there are two divorce decrees, a preliminary one and a final one (see pages 11-12).

3

Making Sure You Are Doing the Right Thing

Is divorce what you really want?

Strange though it may seem, divorce is far more final than getting married – it will put an end to your marriage for ever. Once the final divorce decree is granted the only way you will be able to change your mind will be to get married to your former spouse all over again.

If your marriage is in serious difficulties and you are contemplating divorce, but you are not sure whether it is the right thing to do, you may be feeling isolated and lonely. Even if you are lucky enough to have close friends and family who are supporting you through your troubles, and there to listen when you feel like sharing them, you may want to consider contacting an organisation like *Relate* (formerly known as The Marriage Guidance Council). Their skilled counsellors can help you either to move towards a reconciliation with your spouse, or simply to decide what you really want to do. You do not have to go to *Relate* counselling as a couple – they will see you on your own if that is appropriate. The title of the first chapter of the book *The Relate Guide to Starting Again* by S. Litvinoff is 'Do You Really Want to Break Up?' – you may find it helpful reading if you are in this situation. You will find an address and more information about *Relate* (and many other organisations) in Chapter 26.

Remember that even once the divorce procedure has begun, it is not too late to give your marriage another try. If you and your spouse both want to have another go, you can pause the proceedings for a while (as long as you let your solicitors and the court know) or you can have the divorce petition dismissed (if you are the petitioner). Even once the decree nisi has been made, you can apply to the court to have it rescinded – although once decree absolute has been made your divorce will be final. Surveys show that some people who decided that they wanted a divorce, later wish they were still with their original partners. If you find yourself regretting or feeling uneasy about the decision to divorce before decree absolute, say so.

You may want to live apart from your spouse, without actually getting divorced. You can obtain legal help from the courts of a less radical nature than a divorce. For example, your solicitor will be able to advise you about the courts' powers to sort out particular problems that may have arisen, for instance over money or the children or the occupation of the house, without actually going to the lengths of granting you a divorce. Another alternative that might appeal to those who have objections to a divorce, perhaps on religious grounds, but who still wish to sever all connections with their spouse, is a judicial separation. This puts your separation on a formal basis and enables the court to sort out questions of maintenance and property for you without actually ending your marriage. Or you may wish to consider entering into a separation agreement with your spouse in which you can make arrangements for living apart from each other without getting divorced, or going to court at all.

Once the divorce is over

If you do decide to get divorced, once your divorce comes through you may feel very lonely. You may have to get used to being single all over again, perhaps spending holidays on your own and some weekends not seeing anyone from Friday night to Monday morning. You will have to come to terms with the loss of your partner and you may feel anger or guilt, sadness or depression.

Adjusting to your new life is bound to be difficult, but you may eventually be able to look upon your divorce as a fresh start. You may not feel like initiating social activities, but it will probably be beneficial. There may be interests or hobbies which you neglected while you were married, which you could pursue again now. Or there may be something completely new that you feel like trying. You may find it helpful to get in touch with other people in your situation through various organisations, for example *One Parent Families*. Some people find it helpful to examine – with or without the help of a counsellor (perhaps from an organisation such as *Relate*) – what went wrong in their marriage, to help them avoid making the same mistakes again or repeating the same patterns in future relationships.

Above all, try to avoid looking back and having regrets for the way things might have been – you will be able to make yourself a new life, however small the prospect may seem at the outset.

4

Should You Consult a Solicitor?
The Pros, the Cons and the Cost

There is no compulsion on you to consult a solicitor at any stage of your divorce if you do not want to do so. However, as a general rule, it makes sense to take legal advice about a divorce. Exactly how much help you will require from a solicitor will depend on your own personal preference and the circumstances of your case.

Most divorces involve two stages – the initial step of obtaining the divorce decree (referred to in this chapter as 'the divorce') and the (often much more tricky) problem of making arrangements about the children, family property, maintenance, etc., for the future (referred to in this chapter as 'future arrangements').

1. How can a solicitor help?
a) WITH THE DIVORCE
Some time ago the procedure for obtaining a divorce was simplified so that, in most cases, there is no formal court hearing and most of the divorce can be dealt with by means of paperwork. This was done with the aim of reducing the amount of legal help required by people getting divorced and, provided the circumstances of the case are fairly straightforward, it is now possible to get divorced without ever seeing a solicitor at all.

How do you know if your case is sufficiently straightforward to handle yourself? There is no simple answer to this. It all depends on your personal circumstances and it is unfortunately not impossible for a case that seems clear cut and without problems at the outset to turn into a nightmare (and, of course, vice versa).

As a guide, as a petitioner, you are most likely to be able to handle your own divorce where:

(i) your spouse is content to be divorced and will not be raising any objections to your divorce petition

and (ii) you will be basing your divorce petition on the fact that your spouse has committed *adultery* (which he or she is prepared to admit to the court) or the fact that you have been *separated for two years and your spouse consents* to the divorce or on the fact that you have been *separated for five years* (see Chapter 7 for details of the grounds for divorce).

You may also feel sufficiently confident to look after the case yourself where your spouse is content to be divorced and you intend to base your petition on his or her *behaviour* which you are quite sure is so serious that you cannot be expected to go on living with him or her.

As a respondent, you may find it possible to handle the divorce yourself provided you do not wish to object to the divorce being granted or to anything that your spouse has said about you in the petition and you are certain that you understand fully what the divorce will mean to you.

Anyone who does not fall within these categories will find the help of a solicitor invaluable.

Whilst it may be possible for you to manage without a solicitor, many people feel more comfortable if they do have legal advice. Furthermore, conducting your own divorce proceedings can turn out to be time consuming, and some people simply cannot spare the time to deal with everything themselves.

If you do consult a solicitor, he will take charge of the divorce proceedings for you from obtaining the information that is needed to start the case off to obtaining the final decree of divorce. Although he will almost certainly complete the necessary forms for you, you will still be required to check that they are correct and, from time to time, to sign documents and possibly to deliver them to the court. He will also make sure that, if there is anything the law can do to help you, you do not have to struggle with money problems or difficulties over children, accommodation, the behaviour of your spouse, etc., whilst you are waiting for the divorce to come through.

As you will see from the following section, you will

probably want to consult a solicitor about your future arrangements. One of the advantages of seeing a solicitor about the divorce itself is that he can also get the ball rolling in relation to future arrangements at a very early stage. This should mean that everything can be finalised by agreement between you or by the court with the minimum delay so that you can put your marriage behind you and make a fresh start as soon as possible.

b) WITH FUTURE ARRANGEMENTS

In almost every case, it is prudent (if not essential) to consult a solicitor about your future arrangements.

Some couples are fortunate enough to be able to discuss arrangements for everything with each other amicably. If you are in this position, your solicitor will ensure that the terms you have come to are the best for you in the long run, and will help you to record your agreements in a form that will secure the maximum tax advantage for both of you (if financial arrangements are involved) and that will lead to the least dispute in the future over exactly what was agreed.

If you find that you and your spouse get at each other's throats whenever you try to discuss things, your solicitor can fulfil a valuable role as negotiator for you. He will also advise you what you can reasonably expect by way of capital and maintenance and what you can reasonably be required to provide for your spouse. He will help you to decide what arrangements will be best in relation to the children. With assistance of this kind, you will often find that it is possible to come to a solution that suits both of you without involving the court to decide for you.

If it does become necessary to ask the court to determine your future arrangements for you, your solicitor will take complete charge of the proceedings and, if a court hearing is involved, he will see that all the evidence that supports your case is put before the court and that you are represented during the hearing by either himself or a barrister.

Until the implementation of the Family Law Act 1996, if you could not reach agreement, the only alternative was to go to court. One of the main objectives of the Act was to encourage people to use mediation to resolve issues between them in divorce proceedings. If you want to explore this option, see Chapter 17 of this book, and ask your solicitor.

2. Choosing a solicitor

If you have regularly consulted a solicitor in the past, you will probably want to let him deal with the divorce for you. Not all solicitors deal with matrimonial work, however, nor do they all have a contract with the Legal Services Commission which enables them to provide publicly funded legal advice and representation (see below). If you require help of a type that your existing solicitor cannot give you, he will tell you and he may be able to pass you on to another member of his firm or suggest other firms that you could consult.

It is almost always advisable for you and your spouse to consult different solicitors over the divorce and future arrangements. If you have both consulted the same solicitor in the past, you may be reluctant to change now. If so, ask your solicitor what his view is about representing both of you. He may feel that, in your particular case, he can properly do this. On the other hand, if he feels that you should have separate solicitors, you will have to decide which of you is to seek help elsewhere. You can certainly ask your solicitor to guide you by giving you the names of some other firms who may deal with your case.

If you do not already have a solicitor, it can be a daunting task trying to choose one. If you would like to see a fairly comprehensive list of the firms that work in your area, you can consult such a list at your local Citizens' Advice Bureau or in the Yellow Pages. If you feel there is a possibility that you may be eligible for public funding, it would be a good idea to consult a solicitor who undertakes this type of work from the outset.

The selection of solicitors who provide the services you require will no doubt be bewildering at first. If you know other people who have consulted a solicitor over similar matters, you can ask them if they can recommend him or her. Try to choose a firm that you can conveniently visit from your home or work – you may have to see your solicitor at his office on a number of occasions during the proceedings. Bear in mind the opening hours of the firm that you are considering: most firms work normal office hours so it is unusual to find a firm that is open on a Saturday. If it would be impossible for you to get to see your solicitor during working hours, you might like to investigate what his or her attitude would be to making special arrangements to see you on a Saturday or late in the afternoon.

Once you have decided on a firm of solicitors, telephone them or call in and check that they can give you the sort of help you require. Ask them whether they would be prepared to take on your case and, if a particular solicitor in the firm has been recommended to you, mention that you would like him to deal with your case for you.

3. What will it all cost?

Most people are only reluctant to see a solicitor because they are worried about the cost. In fact, many solicitors will keep their charges to quite a reasonable amount in a divorce case. Furthermore, you may be eligible for help with your legal costs by way of public funding from the Legal Services Commission (formerly known as the 'Legal Aid Board'). This public funding (formerly 'legal aid') exists for the benefit of those who would normally have difficulty in meeting the cost of a solicitor's advice. To operate any of the public funding schemes, solicitors' firms have to be approved by, and have a contract with, the Legal Services Commission. These firms will hold a 'Quality Mark'.

The different types of public funding (described by the Legal Services Commission as 'levels of service') are described below in paragraphs a) – c).

a) LEGAL HELP
(i) *What does Legal Help cover?*
Legal Help covers the work that the solicitor will do in an undefended divorce suit until his charges reach a total of £500. Only the divorce itself will be covered by Legal Help, not the

work needed to deal with financial arrangements or any
dispute over children. For those matters there are other forms
of public funding.

(ii) *Are you eligible?*
Whether you are eligible for assistance will depend on your
means. Both your capital and income will be taken into
account. The financial limits for the schemes will be altered
periodically to keep pace with inflation and each applicant's
individual circumstances are taken into the calculation so it is
not possible to give a definite guide as to whether you will
qualify or not. Having said that, if you are in receipt of Income
Support or Income based Jobseeker's Allowance, you will be
eligible for all types of public funding including funding under
the Legal Help scheme, without having to pay a contribution.
Being properly in receipt of those types of benefit gives you a
sort of 'passport' to public funding.

If you receive another type of benefit or tax credit such as
Working Families' Tax Credit or Disabled Person's Tax
Credit, or your income and capital are not high, you may still
be entitled to assistance. Depending on the figures involved,
you may be required to pay a contribution from your income
or capital. Unless there is in excess of £100,000 equity in the
property, the fact that you are a homeowner will be disre-
garded in assessing your assets.

Information about Legal Help and the current financial
limits should be available from your local Citizens' Advice
Bureau and Law Centre. Alternatively, you can contact the
Legal Services Commission Leafletline on 0845 3000343 or
download the information from the LSC website (see Chapter
26).

When you see your solicitor at the first meeting, he will
work out whether you are eligible for Legal Help. It will help
him to calculate whether you qualify if you take with you
details of your income (wage slips, interest from savings, etc.),
your outgoings (mortgage or rent information, council tax
payments and other bills), and your capital (savings, stocks
and shares, etc.). If you are on any kind of benefit or tax credit,

it will help if you also take details of these. Using this information, he will be able to tell you at once whether you are eligible for Legal Help. Unfortunately, this initial interview will be 'pre-certificate' and (unless you are on Income Support or Income based Jobseeker's Allowance) you will have to pay for it.

Bear in mind that you may be asked at a later date to reimburse the Legal Services Commission (which will have borne the cost of your legal advice up to that point) from any property that you receive from your spouse or manage to retain as part of your arrangements for the future. You should refer to the later part of this chapter headed THE STATUTORY CHARGE: A WORD OF WARNING ABOUT PUBLIC FUNDING for further details of this liability (page 28).

b) APPROVED FAMILY HELP: HELP WITH MEDIATION AND GENERAL FAMILY HELP

(i) *What does Approved Family Help cover?*

As we saw in paragraph a) (i) above, Legal Help does not cover work needed to deal with financial arrangements or disputes over children. To deal with those issues, you will need the next level of service, Approved Family Help, which covers advice and negotiation but not representation in a contested hearing at court. Approved Family Help can take two forms: Help with Mediation or General Family Help.

Help with Mediation covers legal advice to support you if you are participating in Family Mediation – you can find out more about mediation in Chapter 17. If you successfully reach an agreement through mediation, this type of funding can cover the cost of obtaining a court order to confirm the agreement.

Help with Mediation will cover the cost of a solicitor until his charges reach £350 where the issues are about children and finances, £250 where the issues are only about finances, and £150 where the issues are only about children.

To encourage people to use mediation to resolve their disputes, this is the only type of public funding which is completely exempt from the 'statutory charge': in other words, you cannot be required to make contributions or reimburse the Legal Services Commission for this type of funding, whatever your means.

General Family Help covers negotiations where no mediation is in progress, although as with Legal Representation *it will not usually be granted unless a mediator has considered the suitability of your case for mediation* (see page 27, THE NEED TO EXPLORE MEDIATION). If the negotiations lead to an agreement, it can cover obtaining a court order to confirm the agreement.

General Family Help also covers representation if you have to go to court to obtain disclosure of information, for example where your spouse has not been open about his financial situation. If you need representation at court for other types of application, you will usually have to apply for Legal Representation (see paragraph c) below).

Under a certificate for General Family Help, you will be able to get help from a solicitor or adviser until his charges reach an initial limit of £1,500, although this can be extended where necessary on application to the Legal Services Commission.

(ii) *Are you eligible?*

As with Legal Help, whether you qualify for assistance will depend on your capital and income (see paragraph a) (ii) above) although different financial limits apply. If you are receiving income support or income-based jobseeker's allowance, you will automatically be eligible for Help with Mediation and General Family Help.

c) LEGAL REPRESENTATION

(i) *What does Legal Representation cover?*

You may have tried to resolve your disputes with your spouse through mediation and negotiation, but found yourself unable to sort matters out. Going to court may be unavoidable. In those circumstances, you will need to apply for funding under the Legal Representation scheme.

Although the Legal Services Commission can impose conditions or limitations on the extent of funding, in principle

Legal Representation covers all work needed to take your case to court. If you are eligible for this type of funding, your solicitor will receive a certificate setting out the conditions upon which it is granted to you. This will tell him exactly what work he can do for you.

(ii) *Are you eligible?*
The financial conditions which have to be satisfied before you can receive funding under this scheme are similar to those that apply to Help with Mediation and General Family Help.

EMERGENCY APPLICATIONS
Where appropriate (for example, to cover the cost of applying for a domestic violence injunction), Legal Representation can be granted on an emergency basis. If it is, the certificate will cover the first stages of the work that needs doing. However, in making the application you have to promise to make a full application. If on making a full application you find that you are not financially eligible, you will be liable for all the costs of the case. Therefore you should take care to describe very accurately your financial circumstances to your solicitor at the outset.

THE NEED TO EXPLORE MEDIATION
You should be aware that since the Family Law Act 1996 came into force there has been greater emphasis on divorcing couples attempting to resolve their differences themselves through mediation. Previously couples who could not reach an agreement about future arrangements had no alternative but to go to court. Now mediation is available (for further details see Chapter 17).

To encourage you to make use of this facility, the legislation provides a carrot and a stick. An advantage of resolving your issues through mediation rather than court proceedings (the carrot) is that Help with Mediation is not subject to the statutory charge: in other words, you cannot be required to pay that money back. On the other hand, you cannot make an application for Approved Family Help

and/or Legal Representation until you have first explored
whether mediation would be a viable alternative to litigation
in your case (the stick). This rule does not apply to
applications for personal protection or occupation orders
(dealt with in Chapter 12 of this book) or applications for
injunctions to prevent or set aside disposal of property
(Chapter 18).

Even if the *type* of proceedings you are intending to take
does not provide an exception to the general requirement to
attend an initial meeting with a mediator, other circumstances
might make the initial meeting inappropriate in your case. In
particular, if you would be influenced during the mediation
process by fear of violence or other harm from your partner,
you would not be required to attend the initial meeting.
Alternatively, there may be some practical reason why a
meeting would be inappropriate: for example, if you or your
spouse are in hospital and therefore unable to attend. Your
solicitor will ask you about all your circumstances and advise
you on whether your case falls into one of the categories of
exemption.

THE STATUTORY CHARGE: A WORD OF WARNING ABOUT
PUBLIC FUNDING
Beware! Many people think that public funding relieves you
of the responsibility for your solicitor's costs for ever. This is
often not the case.

If, as part of your arrangements for the future after you are
divorced, you receive some capital (be it in the form of the
family home or other assets, or as a lump sum of money) you
can be required to reimburse the Legal Services Commission
from this capital for any of your legal costs that it has had to
bear. This is known as the 'statutory charge'. You can be
liable in this way even if you think that the property you get
has belonged to you all along if your spouse has tried to claim
a share in it at any stage in the divorce proceedings. The first
£3,000 is, at the time of writing, excused from this liability nor
can any claim be made on property which goes to your
children or income which is paid to you as maintenance.

Furthermore, if the property is the matrimonial home or a sum of money intended for the purchase of a house, the statutory charge can be postponed. A charge is then put on the house, and the debt and accrued interest on it is repaid only when the house is sold.

The operation of these provisions can be very complicated and you should ask your solicitor to explain exactly how they may affect you. The Legal Services Commission publishes leaflets about the statutory charge: 'A practical guide to community and legal service funding' and 'Paying back the Legal Services Commission: The Statutory Charge'. You can get these from your solicitor or the LSC website (see Chapter 26). Of course, the exact amount of your costs that the Legal Services Commission has had to bear will depend on how much your solicitor's bill for everything connected with the divorce was, how much you have already paid by way of contribution to your costs, and how much, if anything, you have been able to recover towards your costs from your spouse (see below).

To give you a simple example of how the rules work, suppose that Mr and Mrs X decide to get divorced. Mrs X sees a solicitor and receives advice under the Legal Help scheme. She pays no contribution. The Legal Help scheme pays for all her legal costs in connection with the divorce itself. She and her husband are not able to agree over their house (which is their only capital asset) or over maintenance and Mrs X's solicitor therefore applies for public funding on her behalf. This is granted and again she has no contribution to make. The public funding covers the cost of all the proceedings in relation to the house and maintenance. Finally the court decides for them that Mr X should transfer the house (which is in his name) worth £150,000 and free of mortgage, to Mrs X but pay her no maintenance.

The total bill for Mrs X's legal costs is £2,000 (an arbitrary figure which is not to be taken as a guide to the likely costs in your case). The court decides that, for a variety of reasons that need not concern us, Mr X should not have to pay any of his wife's costs. Therefore, the LSC is out of pocket to the tune of

£2,000. Mrs X has received property worth well over £3,000 and she will therefore be required to reimburse the LSC for the whole £2,000. However, as the capital she gets is tied up in the house, there will be an arrangement called a 'charge' over the house. This is rather like a mortgage in favour of the fund. Mrs X will not have to pay back any of the £2,000 yet. However, when she comes to sell the house, she can be required to pay back the whole £2,000 (plus interest) out of the sale proceeds unless special permission is given for the charge to be carried over onto any new house she buys.

If Mrs X had received, say, £30,000 as a lump sum of money instead of the house, she may have had to meet the £2,000 from this straight away though it may sometimes be possible to arrange for a charge instead where the money is earmarked for the purchase of a new home.

Instead of being asked to reimburse the LSC, you may have the pleasant surprise of receiving a refund of some of the initial contributions you have made towards the cost of your legal advice. This will normally only happen if your spouse is ordered to pay all your costs in relation to the divorce and future arrangements for you. Your solicitor will advise you what your prospects are. Do not rely on getting any money back – it does not usually happen.

WHAT IF YOU ARE NOT ELIGIBLE FOR HELP WITH YOUR SOLICITOR'S COSTS?
What do you do if you discover that you are not able to benefit from any form of assistance with your solicitor's costs? You will then have to decide whether you wish to meet his bill from your own pocket. Do not make this decision without first investigating what he will charge you. In straightforward cases, a solicitor may be able to give you a fairly precise estimate of his charges. In a more complex matter, you can only expect a rough guide. Solicitors are used to being asked about cost and will be as helpful as they can.

In some cases, you may be able to recover at least part of your outlay from your spouse although you should never rely on being able to do so (see below).

Substantial though your solicitor's charges may seem to be, do bear in mind that he can often save you money in the long term by making sure your case runs smoothly and that you secure the arrangements for the future that are best for you.

RECOVERING THE COST OF YOUR LEGAL ADVICE FROM YOUR SPOUSE/CONTRIBUTING TOWARDS YOUR SPOUSE'S LEGAL COSTS

You and your spouse can, of course, come to whatever agreement you like over who is to meet your joint legal costs. However, in the absence of any agreement between you, the court can decide whether one of you should have to meet the other's expenses at any stage of the divorce proceedings. The court's decision always depends very much on the particular circumstances of your case and a book of this kind cannot therefore make any firm predictions as to the likely outcome of your case. Your solicitor may, however, be able to give you some more concrete advice on your own position.

If the court is called upon to decide, for example, where the children are to live, or questions relating to property, it is quite free to make whatever order it feels is reasonable about who is to pay the costs of the particular application to the court, whether or not either of you has been receiving public funding. Whether you will recoup any of your costs or have to contribute towards your spouse's will depend on the attitude you have both taken to the matter in hand, who can be said to have been most successful as a result of the court's decision, how much money you each have, etc., etc.

4. Complaining about or changing your solicitor

Most people will be quite satisfied with the service they receive from their solicitor. A few will have complaints and some may want to know whether they can change to another solicitor.

If you have a complaint about your solicitor, you should first approach the firm about it direct. All solicitors' firms have complaints procedures. If you have already been told what the procedure is in your solicitor's firm, follow that procedure. If not, complain to the senior partner.

Keep a copy of your letter of complaint and any other correspondence. Allow the firm a reasonable amount of time to respond then, if you are still not happy or you would like to talk over with an independent person the problem you are having with your solicitor, you can contact the Law Society's Consumer Complaints Service (formerly known as the Office for the Supervision of Solicitors). This is a body staffed by solicitors and non-solicitors which has been established by the Law Society (the solicitors' professional body) to deal with complaints and enquiries about the service provided by the profession. There is a helpline (details of which can be found in Chapter 26) and explanatory leaflets are available dealing with how to go about complaining, what to do if you think your solicitor's charges are too high, etc. In an extreme case, you may wish to consider changing solicitors.

You can change solicitors whenever you want to if you are meeting all your legal costs out of your own pocket. However, you will have to pay your existing solicitor's bill before he will release the papers in your case to another solicitor and without these papers a new solicitor can really do nothing. Furthermore, you should consider very carefully before changing your solicitor because it can cause delay whilst your new solicitor gets accustomed to your case. You should be absolutely sure that you have good reason to change.

If you are receiving public funding, your right to change solicitors may be rather more limited. You cannot change solicitors simply because you do not like the advice you are given, unless you have reason to believe that the advice is actually wrong. However, if you do have good reason to be seriously dissatisfied, you will normally be able to change to another solicitor. The best way to do this is normally to find another solicitor whom you would like to consult and who is prepared to take your case on. Once you have authorised him to take over the case, he will write to the Legal Services Commission to get permission from them for the change and he will write to your former solicitor telling him what has happened and asking him to send on your papers. He will then be responsible for your case.

5. Should you consult a barrister?

A barrister is a lawyer who has been trained in a slightly different way from a solicitor. You will find that, in the legal world, a barrister is often referred to simply as 'counsel'. His job is usually associated with conducting cases in court but another part of a barrister's job is to advise solicitors and their clients about all sorts of legal problems.

A barrister can never be engaged directly by a member of the public. He has to be instructed to act in a case by a solicitor. It is not necessary to enlist the services of a barrister in a straightforward divorce in connection with obtaining the actual decrees of divorce. However, it is not unusual for a barrister to be instructed in connection with other problems arising in the course of the divorce, for example in relation to the children, property and maintenance. If he thinks it is necessary for you to have a barrister, your solicitor may simply go ahead and instruct a barrister for you, or he may discuss the matter with you.

If you feel personally that you would like a barrister and your solicitor shows no signs of raising the question with you, you are free to ask him about it yourself. However, many cases can be handled very adequately by a solicitor, so be prepared to accept your solicitor's advice if he says you do not need a barrister.

In suitable cases, public funding will meet the cost of a barrister for you. If you are not eligible for that, you will, of course, have to meet the barrister's fees yourself. It is wise to ask your solicitor for an estimate of what these are likely to be in advance so that you are not taken by surprise when the bill arrives.

There are a number of senior barristers called 'Queen's Counsel' who are sometimes engaged in more difficult cases. It is hardly ever necessary to instruct a Queen's Counsel (or 'silk') in a divorce case, but if it were to become necessary, your solicitor would ensure that this was done for you. You will usually find that if a Queen's Counsel is instructed, another less senior barrister is also instructed to assist him.

If a barrister is instructed in your case, he may wish to meet you to discuss matters with you. This meeting is usually called a 'conference' and usually takes place at the barrister's chambers (his office) or at the court where your case is to be heard.

5

Can You Get Your Divorce Through the English Courts?

England and Wales are treated as a single country for legal purposes. Scotland and Northern Ireland are separate countries and have laws that differ from those of England and Wales in many respects. 'England' is used in this chapter as a shorthand term for the whole area of England and Wales and the term 'English courts' refers to all courts throughout England and Wales.

The English divorce courts can only deal with your divorce if one or the other of you has some connection with England. You will have sufficient link with England if either:

a) one of you is *domiciled* in England at the time when the divorce proceedings are commenced. Domicile is a legal term for a particularly close relationship between a person and a country. Your domicile is not necessarily the same as your nationality – there are complex rules for determining where you are domiciled at a given time. However, you can take it that, as a general rule, you are domiciled in the country where you have your permanent home and intend to live for an unlimited period of time. Most people who live in England are also domiciled here. But if both of you have or have had a close connection with another country (even with Scotland or Northern Ireland) which amounts to more than just taking regular holidays there, you would be well advised to consult a solicitor to check on your domiciles before embarking on divorce proceedings in the English courts, unless you are quite satisfied that one of you will be able to fulfil the conditions set out in paragraph (b) below:

or (b) one of you will have been *habitually resident* in England for at least one year by the time your divorce proceedings are commenced. Leaving England for short periods, for example on a business trip or for a holiday, will not normally prevent you from being habitually resident here provided you can show that you have, at least, put down some roots here and made this your home for the year.

Provided that one of you can satisfy the domicile or habitual residence conditions, it will not matter where you got married be it in England or the other side of the world – the English courts can still grant you a divorce. An English divorce will effectively put an end to your marriage, certainly as far as your status in this country is concerned. However, if you are worried about the effect of an English divorce on your marital status in another country, it would be wise to check whether that country accepts an English divorce as valid or not. Your solicitor may be able to help, but if not, the embassy of the country in question may provide the information you require.

6

What to Expect When You Come into Contact with the Courts

There is no special family court. Most divorces are dealt with entirely by a branch of the county court system known as the divorce county courts.

The divorce county courts and Family Hearing Centres

County courts are locally based courts that can be found in many towns and cities throughout England and Wales. They do not deal with crimes but they do resolve almost every other type of problem that can arise in everyday life, for example disputes between shopkeepers and dissatisfied customers, between neighbours, between landlords and their tenants, etc.

Not all county courts deal with divorce cases – those that do are known as the divorce county courts. Divorce county courts deal with the administrative side of divorce proceedings only. Contested applications about financial matters, children, etc., will be transferred to a county court which is classed as a Family Hearing Centre.

The work of deciding cases and making court orders is carried out by judges and district judges. Both judges and district judges are appointed from the ranks of senior lawyers. The chances are that most of the court orders that are made in the course of your divorce will be made by a district judge. You may meet him personally once or twice during the case, for example if you ask the court to sort out what should happen to your property for you or to determine whether you should be paying or receiving maintenance. If you have problems over your children, this aspect of your case may have to be dealt with by a judge.

There is also a large staff of court officials who are responsible for the smooth running of the court's business. Some of them are employed in the court office attached to

most courts, where they deal with all the paperwork involved
in county court cases. You will meet one or two of them if you
attend the court office for any reason and you will normally
find them very friendly and helpful with any queries you may
have. Other members of the staff are more directly involved in
the day to day organisation of the court, ensuring that the court
has just the right amount of business lined up to deal with each
day (insofar as this is possible), checking that you, and
everyone else involved in the court proceedings, are in the
right place at the right time and know what you should be
doing, making sure that the judge has all the papers he needs
to deal with each case, etc. You may meet some of these
officials, particularly the court clerk and the ushers, if you
have to attend court for a hearing.

In London the equivalent of the divorce county court is the
divorce registry, which is situated in the Royal Courts of
Justice in the Strand.

The offices of the divorce county courts and the divorce
registry are normally open on weekdays from about 10 a.m.
until approximately 4 p.m. or 4.30 p.m. The courts usually
hold their hearings (or 'sit') between similar hours.

The High Court
Occasionally it is necessary for a particularly difficult question
that arises in a divorce case to be referred to the High Court.
There are several sections of the High Court – the section
responsible for divorce and other similar matters is called the
Family Division.

The High Court is based in London, but this does not mean
you will have to travel to London if your case is referred to the
High Court. Judges of the High Court regularly visit major
towns and cities throughout England and Wales to deal with
cases that arise outside the London area.

The format of court hearings
Hearings connected with a divorce are dealt with either in
'open court' or in 'chambers'.

Proceedings in open court are heard in the courtroom itself.

They tend to be rather formal and all the lawyers concerned will wear their legal robes for the occasion. Members of the public are normally permitted to come into court and listen to the case if they wish to do so, and the details can be reported in the press. The only matter which is likely to be dealt with in open court in the course of your divorce is the pronouncement of decree nisi of divorce – you need not usually attend for this if you would prefer not to.

Most of the divorce will be dealt with in chambers. Proceedings in chambers are heard in private, either in the courtroom itself or in the judge's or the district judge's own room at the court. The general public has no right to listen to any part of the case and no details can be reported in the press. Only those people who are directly concerned in the case are allowed to be present – this often means just you, your spouse, your legal advisers and the court staff. Hearings in chambers tend to be less formal and more relaxed than open court hearings and the lawyers involved will not be wearing robes.

PART 2:
THE DIVORCE ITSELF

7
Do You Qualify for a Divorce?

A divorce can only be obtained through the courts. There are certain basic legal requirements that must be satisfied before you can be granted a divorce. These are outlined below.

1. Divorce within the first year of marriage
Marriage often means a great change in life style and it can take quite a while to get used to. You could be tempted to decide in the early days that you have made a serious mistake and to start thinking of a divorce at once. To make sure that you do not rush out of your marriage without giving it a fair chance of success, the law provides that no one can apply for a divorce until they have been married for one year, even if they have grounds for a divorce.

IS THERE ANY HELP I CAN GET IN THE FIRST YEAR OF MARRIAGE?
The restriction on filing a petition within the first year of marriage only applies to proceedings for divorce. In a suitable case you may be able to start proceedings to have your marriage annulled (for example if your spouse has refused to consummate it) or for a decree of judicial separation (which does not dissolve your marriage but simply places the court's seal of approval on your living apart) at any stage after your marriage. You will find brief details about your rights in this respect in Chapter 2. If you require personal protection from your spouse, or financial help or assistance over your house or in relation to your children, there are several ways of obtaining such assistance from the courts without seeking a divorce;

there is no need for you to have been married for any particular length of time before you seek help. You will be able to find out more about this type of thing in the chapters dealing with the appropriate topics later in this book. However, it is not possible in a book of this size to give sufficient information to satisfy everybody's needs so, if you need help, consult a solicitor for advice on your rights, even if you do not think you would be eligible to petition for a divorce yet.

2. The grounds for divorce

If you have been married for at least a year, and the court has jurisdiction, you will be eligible for a divorce if you can satisfy the court that you fulfil certain basic legal requirements.

(i) JURISDICTION

Either you or your spouse, or both of you, must be living in or have your permanent homes ('domicile') in England or Wales (see Chapter 5 for more detail). If there is any doubt about either of your habitual residence or domicile, you will need to consult a solicitor about this.

(ii) IRRETRIEVABLE BREAKDOWN OF THE MARRIAGE

The court will only be prepared to grant a divorce if it is satisfied that your marriage has broken down irretrievably, or in other words, that it is finally over and there is no possibility of you and your spouse getting back together again.

Quite frequently one spouse would like the marriage to continue but the other is adamant that it is at an end. Obviously, if there is to be any real prospect of a reconciliation, both spouses have to be prepared to give the marriage another chance. If one spouse is not willing to do this and the court is satisfied that this is a definite and final refusal, it will accept that the marriage has broken down irretrievably.

(iii) THE FIVE FACTS

To prove that the marriage has broken down irretrievably, you will have to prove one of the following five facts to the court:

a) that the respondent has committed adultery and you find it intolerable to live with him or her (commonly referred to simply as 'adultery');

b) that the respondent has behaved in such a way that you cannot reasonably be expected to live with him or her ('unreasonable behaviour');

c) that the respondent has deserted you for a continuous period of at least two years immediately before the presentation of your petition for divorce ('desertion');

d) that you have lived apart for a continuous period of at least two years immediately preceding the presentation of your petition and that the respondent consents to a divorce ('two years' separation and consent');

e) that you have lived apart for a continuous period of at least five years immediately preceding the presentation of your petition ('five years' separation').

These facts are explained in more detail below.

a) ADULTERY

The adultery itself

A man has committed adultery if he has had sexual intercourse with another woman (married or unmarried) whilst he is married to his wife. A married woman commits adultery if she has sexual intercourse voluntarily with a man other than her husband. Because it is essential that the sexual intercourse should be a voluntary act, a woman who is raped does not commit adultery. A sexual relationship outside the marriage that does not actually involve sexual intercourse is not adultery, although it may be unreasonable behaviour of a kind that would entitle the other spouse to petition for a divorce (see below).

You are most unlikely to catch your spouse in the act of committing adultery. Nevertheless you will be expected to prove to the court that he has done so. In many cases, he will be prepared to admit that he has committed adultery and this makes your task quite straightforward. The court can be informed of the respondent's admission very simply. When he first receives the divorce papers from the court, he will also be sent a form of questionnaire called an acknowledgement of service. One of the questions on the form asks him if he admits that he has committed adultery. If he answers this question affirmatively, the court may be prepared to accept this as sufficient proof.

If the respondent is not prepared to admit adultery, your task may be considerably harder. You will have to produce evidence to the court proving that he has committed adultery. In this situation it is quite common for an enquiry agent (private detective) to be engaged to keep watch on the respondent. The enquiry agent can then inform the court of any circumstances that strongly suggest that adultery has taken place, for example he may be able to give evidence that the respondent spent the night alone with another woman at her house, or that the respondent and another woman booked into a hotel as 'Mr and Mrs Such and Such', taking only one double bedded room.

Sometimes it is not necessary to instruct an enquiry agent at all because you are already in possession of evidence that strongly points to adultery. For example, you may have found correspondence between your husband or wife and another woman or man in terms that make it clear they have been having a sexual relationship, or you may have discovered that your husband or wife is in possession of contraceptives that you know he or she never uses when you have sexual intercourse together. In the case of a wife, it may be possible to prove that she has become pregnant at a time when you could not have had sexual intercourse with her, perhaps because you were away on a prolonged business trip, or ill in hospital. Obviously, the evidence available will be different in each case – these are just examples to give you an idea of the type of evidence that the courts normally expect.

The name of the other man or woman involved in the adultery may be given in the divorce petition. If you mention the name of the other person involved in the adultery in your petition, that person is entitled to take part in the divorce proceedings in so far as they affect him or her. The proper term for such a person would then be the 'co-respondent'. The court will provide the co-respondent with copies of all the relevant divorce papers and he or she will have the opportunity to confirm or deny anything said about him or her in the divorce proceedings. However, you do not have to name the co-respondent. You can simply state on the petition that the respondent 'has committed adultery with [a man or woman] whose name and identity are unknown to the petitioner'.

Proving that it is intolerable for you to live with the respondent

Proving the adultery is only the first step. You have to go on to satisfy the court that you find it intolerable to live with the respondent any more. Strange though it may seem, it is not essential that you find it intolerable to live with the respondent *because* of his adultery. Of course, in many cases the two things are bound up together. On the other hand, it may be that your marriage has been unhappy for some time before the adultery takes place and everything has combined to make it intolerable for you to go on living with the respondent.

Living together after you find out about the adultery

If, after you find out about the respondent's adultery, you live together as man and wife for a period exceeding six months, or for several periods which together add up to more than six months, you will not be able to rely on that adultery to obtain a divorce. This is not to say that you cannot make attempts at a reconciliation: as long as the period or periods during which you live together do not exceed six months in total, the court will completely disregard them in considering whether you should be granted a divorce. Furthermore, a new six month period will be allowed after each fresh act of adultery is discovered.

So, suppose that at the beginning of 2004, you discover that your husband has been committing adultery with Samantha Bloggs but you nevertheless go on living with him as his wife for the whole of 2004 – you would not be able to rely on this adultery in seeking a divorce. However, if you were to discover in, say, January 2005 that your husband committed adultery again in December 2004 with Samantha Bloggs or with any other woman, you would be allowed a further six months living with your husband before you would lose your right to claim a divorce based on the December 2004 adultery.

b) UNREASONABLE BEHAVIOUR

The behaviour

Although people have generally come to talk about getting a divorce because of their spouse's 'unreasonable behaviour' (and the term is also used in this book), this is not strictly an accurate description of the type of conduct that must be proved before a divorce can be obtained. The law actually says that you must show that your spouse has behaved in such a way that you cannot reasonably be expected to live with him or her. The court will make an individual judgment in your case as to whether you should have to go on putting up with your spouse's behaviour. The final decision will depend on what sort of people you both are and on all the circumstances of your case.

It is not possible to lay down hard and fast rules about the type of behaviour that will and will not justify a divorce.

However, as a guide to the sort of standard that the court will apply, it is not sufficient that you simply do not get on with your husband or wife any more or that you have come to the conclusion that you are incompatible. It is only when the behaviour of your spouse goes beyond the ordinary wear and tear of married life and begins to cause serious problems in the home that the court will step in to grant a divorce.

There are a number of types of behaviour that frequently crop up in some shape or form as unreasonable behaviour. They range from violence and threats of violence to persistent abuse, nagging, drunkenness, neglect, refusing to have sexual relations, indulging in sexual perversions, associations with other men or women outside the marriage, placing unreasonable restrictions on the personal freedom of the other spouse, failing to provide the other spouse with sufficient money, etc.,

etc. In some cases, even relatively trivial incidents can be too much to expect a husband or wife to put up with if they happen repeatedly during the marriage.

How do you judge whether you can be expected to go on living with your spouse? It is easy to lose all sense of proportion when your marriage is breaking down and to take it for granted that the reason for all your problems is that your spouse is behaving in an unreasonable manner. However, it is not sufficient that you personally think so – you have got to satisfy the court as well. It may help you to look at your situation rationally if you ask yourself these two simple questions:

'Would an outsider who did not know me or my spouse think that my spouse was behaving towards me in such an unreasonable manner that I should not be expected to have to go on living with him/her?' If your answer to this first question is 'Yes', then the conduct of which you complain may well be serious enough for you to obtain a divorce. If your truthful answer is 'No', you should ask yourself a second question:

'Is there anything out of the ordinary about me or my spouse or our particular circumstances that makes my spouse's behaviour unreasonable though it would not be in most cases?' If you can answer this question affirmatively, then you may still be entitled to a divorce because the court will be prepared to take into account the personalities of yourself and your spouse.

To take an extreme example, suppose that you are a very confident person and very keen on insisting on your rights. You may think it perfectly right that your husband complains in a loud voice in public places whenever the smallest detail does not meet with his complete satisfaction. Indeed you may find it excessively irritating if your husband was not prepared to speak up in this way. But, if you are a very shy and retiring person, you may find this type of behaviour quite unbearable and extremely upsetting and the court would bear this in mind. If, on top of your own character, you could show that your husband behaved in this way largely in order to upset you, you may find that the court would be ready to accept that you should not have to go on living with him and to grant you a divorce. Of course, things can also work the other way and the circumstances of the particular marriage can turn conduct that would otherwise be unreasonable into conduct that is understandable and acceptable.

To take another example, let us suppose that both husband and wife are Catholics. The wife, being very anxious not to become pregnant again, insists on using contraceptives when they have sexual intercourse. The husband, on religious grounds, feels that this is wrong and refuses to have sexual intercourse with her at all in these circumstances. In some cases, an outright refusal to have sexual intercourse could be regarded as unreasonable behaviour. But in the light of the husband's religious beliefs, the court may well accept that he is not in fact being unreasonable.

The fact that the respondent's behaviour is caused by an illness from which he is suffering will not necessarily prevent it from being unreasonable, although the court would normally expect that, up to a point, you should accept and share the burdens imposed on the family by the physical or mental ill health of one spouse.

For one spouse simply to leave the other would not normally amount to unreasonable behaviour. (Although in such a case it may be appropriate to seek a divorce on the basis of a period of separation or desertion – see the following paragraphs.) However, if the departure is accompanied by other unpleasant conduct, the court may be prepared to decide that you cannot be expected to live with the respondent in the future and to grant you a divorce.

Does it matter that we are still living together?

As with adultery, your right to claim that you cannot be expected to go on living with your spouse will not be affected by the fact that you have, in fact, lived with him whilst the behaviour of which you complain was taking place or even after it occurred, *provided* that the period (or periods) during which you live together do not total more than six months. If you live together as man and wife for a period (or periods) in excess of six months after the last incident of which you complain, you will have to explain in your affidavit the reasons why (for example, you may have had to do so because you were unable to find alternative accommodation), or explain that you have not lived as husband and wife and have in effect had two separate households.

c) DESERTION

Proving that your spouse has deserted you for a continuous period of at least two years immediately before you petition for divorce can be a very complicated matter. The following paragraphs will give you a broad outline of what is involved; if you are seeking a divorce on the basis of desertion, your solicitor will check that you can comply with the rather complex legal requirements upon which the court will insist before granting you a decree.

Fortunately it is not often necessary to rely on the fact that your spouse has deserted you when you seek a divorce. This is because desertion often happens as a result of other problems that have arisen in a marriage and there is therefore usually another basis on which a divorce can be granted.

For example, if your spouse has deserted you and you have been separated for at least two years, there is a good chance that he too will have decided that he would like a divorce – if so, you will be able to obtain your divorce on the basis of your two years' separation and his consent to the decree. Or your spouse may have deserted you after behaving unreasonably for some time, in which case you will be able to obtain your divorce by satisfying the court that he has behaved in such a way that you cannot be expected to go on living with him any more. If you find yourself able to prove this, you will not even have to wait for two years' separation to elapse before pressing on with divorce proceedings.

Another quite common reason for one spouse to leave the other is that he or she has found someone else and wishes to set up home with them. Here again, you, as the deserted partner, will not have to wait for two years to pass before taking divorce proceedings as you may well be able to prove that your spouse has committed adultery and obtain a divorce on this basis straight away.

What is desertion?

The simplest form of desertion is when one spouse simply walks out on the other spouse one day for no reason at all. However, desertion is not just a physical separation of husband and wife. It implies that the deserting spouse has completely rejected all the normal obligations of marriage. This means that the court will have to be satisfied of the following things:

(i) two years living separately – you must show that you and your spouse have been living separately for a continuous period of two years immediately before you started the divorce proceedings. Usually the separation comes about when one of you leaves home, but the situation can arise when you are living separately even though you are both still living under the same roof. This will be the case if one of you cuts yourself off completely from the other so that you are no longer living as a married couple. The court is very strict in deciding whether you have reached this state of affairs and will need to be satisfied that you no longer do any of the things together or for each other that married couples normally do, such as eating together, spending your leisure time together, carrying on a sexual relationship, sleeping in the same bed, cooking and washing and doing odd jobs for each other, etc. (This principle is also adopted under (d) below in determining separation for the following ground, two years' separation and consent.)

Although the law requires that you should have been separated for a continuous period of two years, it would be wrong to discourage you from trying to patch things up in the meantime if you wish to do so. Therefore, the court generally disregards short periods during the separation, during which you have lived as man and wife again in an attempt at reconciliation. However, you will not be able to count such periods as part of the two years' separation that you will have to show before you can get your divorce.

So, for example, suppose that a year after you first separated, you spend a month living together again in an attempt to make a success of your marriage again. It is no better than before however and you part again. The month you have spent together will not normally prevent you from starting to count your two years' separation from the time your spouse first deserted you. On the other hand, you cannot count it as *part* of the required two years and you will therefore have to wait until two years and one month have passed from the date of the first desertion before you can seek your divorce.

If, on the other hand, you live together for a period or periods totalling more than six months at any stage after your first separation, the court will be able to take this into account in deciding whether you can establish the relevant period of desertion and the chances are that you will not therefore be able to obtain your divorce on this basis or at least not without encountering further delay.

(ii) that your spouse has decided that the marriage is over – you must also show that when he stopped living with you, your spouse viewed the marriage as ended and intended to remain separated from you permanently. This will often be clear from the way he behaved or from things he said at the time. It means that there will be no desertion where, for example, your spouse only intends a temporary separation or where he still looks upon himself as a married man but has to go away for some reason, for instance because of his job.

You will *not* be able to complain that your spouse has deserted you if:

(i) you consented to the separation – the mere fact that you breathe a sigh of relief as soon as the door closes behind your husband or wife does not mean that you have given your consent to the separation. But in some cases, you may be taken to have consented even though you never actually discussed the matter with your spouse or gave your consent in so many words. This could happen if you have made it clear from your comments or your behaviour that you are agreeable to the separation. This means, for example, that if you ask your husband to leave and he does so or if you decide between you that you should live apart, you will not be able to turn round later and complain that he has deserted you.

(ii) your spouse had good reason to leave – there may be a perfectly acceptable or necessary reason for your spouse leaving, for instance he or she may have had to go into hospital for long term treatment or may even be committed to prison for a criminal offence. This would not be desertion unless your spouse also looked upon the marriage as finished and never intended to come back to you even when he or she was able to do so.

How does desertion end?

In some cases, your spouse's desertion will come to an end and you will no longer be able to rely on it claiming a divorce. This will happen if you get back together again on a permanent basis. Because desertion is a state of affairs that only exists when the separation is against your will, it is also true that if you change your mind and come round to the idea of living apart, and you and your spouse actually come to an agreement that this is what you will do in the future (possibly by drawing up a separation agreement), you will no longer be able to complain that he has deserted you.

d) TWO YEARS' SEPARATION AND CONSENT

If you wish to rely on this basis for your divorce, you will have to prove that you and your spouse have been living apart for a continuous period of two years, just as you must show this if you wish to claim a divorce on the basis that your spouse has deserted you.

The separation

The circumstances in which the law looks upon you as having been separated for the requisite period can include not only periods when you are living in separate places but also times when you are living in the same house but in two separate households, and are more fully described on page 49 under the heading 'What is desertion? . . . (i) two years *living separately'*. Short periods during which you live together will not affect the continuity of your separation provided that they do not exceed six months in total. However, just as with desertion, you will not be able to count these periods towards the two years' separation required. If you live together for a period or periods totalling more than six months, you will not be able to rely on any period of separation that preceded your cohabitation as justifying a divorce, and, if you separate again, you will then have to wait for a further two years to elapse before you can seek a divorce unless you have other grounds for claiming a divorce (adultery or unreasonable behaviour).

At first glance, you may wonder whether there is any difference between two years' separation and consent, and desertion. The most obvious difference is, of course, that you will not be granted a divorce on the basis of two years' separation that does not amount to desertion unless your spouse is prepared to give his consent to the divorce; whereas, if you can show that he deserted you, you can obtain your divorce whether he agrees to it or not.

Why should there be this extra requirement of consent? The reason is that desertion is based on the idea that your spouse has been at fault in separating from you and that you are therefore entitled to a divorce irrespective of his feelings about the matter.

On the other hand, if you can satisfy the court that you both want the divorce, all it will need to know is that you, or one of you, made a decision at some stage that the marriage was over and you were going to part for good, and that since then you have lived separately for at least two years – no question of blame comes into it and you will get your divorce even if you were both fully in agreement about the separation. The type of separation that will never be enough for a divorce is the sort of situation where you both intend to start living together again as soon as you can do so in the future – this will rule out, for example, most separations that come about for reasons simply of business, ill health and imprisonment.

The consent

There are strict rules about proving that your spouse consents to the divorce. It is not enough that, when you ask the court for the divorce, he raises no objections – he must actually signify his consent to the court. His consent will only be valid if he gives it quite freely without any pressure being brought to bear on him and with full understanding of what the divorce will mean to him.

He will normally find it convenient to tell the court of his consent when he completes the questionnaire known as the acknowledgement of service which the court will send him as soon as you have started divorce proceedings. The court also sends a set of notes with the acknowledgement of service form, which explain clearly the consequences of giving consent to the divorce and what the granting of a divorce means. The form is simple to fill in and all your spouse is required to do to give consent is to answer affirmatively the question asking whether he consents to a divorce being granted, sign the form and return it to the court.

If your spouse will not consent to the divorce and you cannot prove that he or she has deserted you (or committed adultery or behaved unreasonably), you will have no choice but to wait until five years' separation has elapsed before you seek a divorce (see below).

If you are the respondent in a divorce of this type, you should be quite sure that you do understand what a divorce will mean to you personally before you give your consent. Even after you have signified your consent to the court, you are free to withdraw it again without any explanation at any stage before the preliminary divorce decree, decree nisi, is pronounced but it is vital to inform the court (and preferably your spouse as well) if you intend to do this. Between decree nisi and decree absolute of divorce you will only be able to withdraw your consent in quite exceptional circumstances. After decree absolute has been obtained, the divorce is final and you will no longer be able to withdraw your consent.

Special protection for respondents

In relation to divorces granted on the basis of two years' separation and consent and five years' separation (see below), the courts have special powers to protect the financial and personal position of the respondent and they can sometimes delay or even prevent the granting of a divorce to make sure that he or she will not suffer because of it.

Generally

A divorce based on two years' separation and consent should present very few problems to either spouse. Many people do seek their divorces on this basis and it is the nearest we have come, in this country, to divorce by mutual consent. It has the great advantage that neither of you has to show that the other has been to blame in any way for the breakdown of the marriage.

e) FIVE YEARS' SEPARATION

If the separation between you has gone on for five years or more, the court will grant you a divorce whether or not your spouse is prepared to agree to it. Apart from the longer period of the separation and the fact that consent is not required, the case will be exactly like that described above based on two years' separation. The court will look upon you as living separately in exactly the same circumstances and you will be able to live together for short periods (not totalling more than six months) without breaking the continuity of the five year period in just the same way.

Should you live together for more than six months, the five year period will only start to clock up once you separate again – you will not be allowed to rely on any time that preceded your cohabitation.

8

Starting the Divorce Proceedings

Your first visit to the solicitor

Each solicitor develops his or her own methods and style over the years so everyone will find their first interview slightly different. (Your solicitor is just as likely to be a woman but for ease of reference 'he' is used, to include both.) It may simply be a preliminary chat that gives you a chance to meet the solicitor and gives him the opportunity to find out roughly what you will need help and advice on. If so, you will probably be asked to make another appointment for some time in the near future so that you can discuss your situation with your solicitor in more detail. On the other hand, some solicitors prefer to get down to business straight away and may spend an hour or so with you, taking down information about your case and giving you a run down of what to expect in the divorce proceedings. It is always a good idea to leave yourself plenty of time for this first visit so that you can relax and take in everything your solicitor says and ask him about anything that is troubling you.

There are certain things that almost every solicitor will do at your first or second appointment:

DEALING WITH THE COST OF YOUR LEGAL ADVICE

a) If he thinks you may be eligible for help under the Legal Help scheme (see Chapter 4), one of the first things he will do is to assess whether you qualify. He will need to ask you about your finances in order to do this, so you can help him if you look out details of your income (from employment, etc.) and your capital (savings in cash or the bank, etc., premium bonds, stocks or shares, etc.) before your first appointment so that you are able to answer his questions accurately and precisely. If you are eligible for help with your legal costs under this scheme, he will tell you straight away. You will be asked to sign the application form he has filled in for you.

b) If you do not qualify for assistance under the Legal Help scheme, you will be able to ask about the cost of legal advice so that you can decide whether you wish to pay for legal help yourself. If you decide to do so, you can tell your solicitor that you would like him to act for you and you can sort out how much money he will require you to pay in advance.

c) If your solicitor thinks you may be eligible for help with your legal costs by way of public funding from the Legal Services Commission (see Chapter 4), he will have to fill in an application form for you at some stage. He may well decide to do so soon after you first consult him to avoid delays later on. This will enable him to get the application off for processing in good time, and you will hear in several weeks' time whether you have been granted public funding or not and how much you will be required to contribute yourself.

FINDING OUT ABOUT YOU AND YOUR MARRIAGE

a) You will be asked to give various details of your marriage, for example, where and when it took place, how many children you have and when they were born, when and where you last lived with your husband or wife, whether there have ever been any other court proceedings in relation to your marriage or your children (for example, you may have made an application in the magistrates' court for maintenance in the past, or perhaps one of your children was adopted by you). If you have a copy of your marriage certificate, it can be helpful if you take it to your solicitor, but if you do not have one, don't worry – your solicitor will help you to get hold of one.

b) Your solicitor will need to know what complaints you are making about your marriage and why you want a divorce, for example because your spouse has committed adultery and you cannot bear to go on living with him or her or because your spouse has behaved so unreasonably that you cannot go on living with him or her.

c) You may well be asked about your own and your spouse's financial position – how much capital do you both have, what do you each earn, is your spouse giving you anything towards your own and the children's expenses or are you giving him or her any money, can you manage on what you have, etc?

Your solicitor is also likely to ask you about the matrimonial home and whether you have come to any agreement about who should live there at present and what should happen to it once the divorce comes through. There are a lot of things a solicitor can do to help with accommodation and money in the early stages of a divorce (for example, by explaining what state benefits might be available to you, or by making an application to the court for an order that your spouse should pay you a regular sum of maintenance until the divorce takes effect). If you feel you need help with anything, therefore, raise it with him as soon as possible, even if he does not raise the point himself. Tell him also if you are in difficulties over the children or if your spouse is harassing you in any way; he may be able to resolve problems of this kind for you too. (You can get a picture of the sort of thing that can be done from the later chapters of this book.)

d) You will be expected to provide an address at which your spouse can be contacted so that he can be notified of the divorce proceedings and sent all the relevant divorce papers. You may not know where your spouse is living – this is not usually a major obstacle as your solicitor will be able to take steps to trace him or, if this proves impossible, he can often make arrangements for the divorce to go ahead nevertheless.

PUTTING YOU IN THE PICTURE

a) Once he has all the information that he needs from you, your solicitor will be able to advise you whether you have grounds for a divorce. If you do, he will tell you something about the procedure involved in obtaining a divorce and he may be able to give you an idea of how long it is likely to take before decree nisi of divorce comes through. If there are any details you particularly want to know, do not be afraid to ask.

b) If your solicitor discovers that you do not yet have grounds for a divorce, he will be able to advise you what alternatives are available to help with your particular problems.

c) You may well be advised that it is best, once you have finally decided on a divorce, if you try to live completely separately from your spouse (for example, you should no longer be sleeping with him, cooking for him, eating with him, etc.). This is just to make sure that you do not prejudice your chances of getting a divorce.

The preparation of the divorce petition and the statement as to the arrangements for the children

a) THE DIVORCE PETITION

Once your solicitor has all the details he requires, he will be able to get on with the next step – preparing the divorce petition. A divorce petition is required in every case. It is the formal legal document that will form the basis of your claim for a divorce. Your solicitor will set down in it details of your marriage and your children and the grounds on which you are seeking a divorce and he will list the claims that you will be asking the court to consider (for example, you may want the court to deal with financial matters for you or to order that the children should reside with you). Your present address will be included in the petition as a matter of course. If you are seriously anxious that you will be in danger if your spouse finds out in this way where you are living, mention this to your solicitor so that he can advise you whether a special application to the court for permission to leave your address out of the petition would be in order in your case.

When your solicitor has drafted the petition, he will ask you to read through it to check that all the information he has included is correct. It is most important that you are very careful about this because it can cause serious problems and delay if information later turns out to be inaccurate and the petition needs correcting.

b) THE STATEMENT OF ARRANGEMENTS

If there is a child or children of your family, another document, known as the 'statement of arrangements for children' (or simply the 'statement of arrangements'), will also have to be prepared at this stage. This sets out the arrangements you propose for the children once the divorce is granted.

A 'child of the family' is any child who is a child of both of you, or who has been adopted legally by both of you, or any other child who has been treated by both of you as part of the family (except a child boarded out with you by a local authority or voluntary organisation). Generally the court is not concerned in divorce proceedings with adult children who can take care of themselves, and you will not have to give any details of the arrangements (if any) for them. But you will be required to provide details of the arrangements for any children who are under 16, or who are under 18 and are still receiving instruction at an educational establishment or undergoing training for a trade or profession (whether or not they are in paid employment as well).

You will need to have information available for your solicitor about any arrangements you have made so far as to where the children are to live, who else will be living there with them, who will look after them, where they are to be educated, what financial arrangements are proposed for them, what arrangements have been made for the other parent to see them (or for you to see them, if they are to live with your spouse), whether they have any illnesses or disability and whether they are under the care or supervision of any person or organisation such as social services.

When your solicitor has filled in the statement of arrangements from these details, he will ask you to check it through for errors and sign it. You should try to reach agreement with your spouse over the arrangements you propose. There is a space at the end of the form for him to sign if he is in agreement; if he does not agree, he will have an opportunity at a later stage to say why not and to make his own proposals (see Chapter 10).

Filing the necessary papers in the court office

Divorce proceedings are actually started by filing (or formally presenting) the appropriate documents at the office of a divorce court. The court office will require:

a) the completed divorce petition (and a copy for your spouse);

b) the completed statement of arrangements, if you have any children of your family of the relevant ages (and a copy for your spouse);

c) a copy of your marriage certificate – your solicitor will tell you how best to obtain one if you have not got a copy;

d) a fee for starting the proceedings.

Once the court receives the documents, it will give your case a reference number. The divorce proceedings are now under way.

9

Obtaining Decree Nisi

The court now takes charge of proceedings for a while. In most cases, the court will address all communications about your case to your solicitor and he will inform you about the progress that is being made.

1. Serving the papers on the respondent (and co-respondent)

Once the petition and accompanying documents have been filed with the court, the court office sends a copy of the petition and the statement of arrangements (if appropriate) to the respondent. This process is described as 'serving' the documents on the respondent. He will also receive two further forms from the court with the divorce papers – the 'acknowledgement of service' and the 'notice of proceedings'.

a) THE NOTICE OF PROCEEDINGS

This informs the respondent that divorce proceedings have been commenced against him and explains that he must return the completed acknowledgement of service form within seven days. He is warned that if he intends to instruct a solicitor, he should take all the divorce papers to the solicitor of his choice who will complete and return the acknowledgement of service for him. It also gives him instructions to assist him in filling in the acknowledgement of service himself if he does not wish to consult a solicitor.

b) THE ACKNOWLEDGEMENT OF SERVICE

This is a document in question and answer form which is primarily designed to enable the court to be certain that the respondent has been served with the divorce papers and is fully aware of the divorce proceedings. The court will not proceed with your case until it is sure that, if it is possible to notify the respondent, he does know that proceedings have been commenced and has details of the proceedings. The respondent is required to confirm on the form that he has received the divorce petition. He is also required to answer questions about his attitude to the divorce, in particular whether he intends to defend the case, whether he objects to paying the costs of the proceedings and whether he intends to make any applications in respect of the children.

If you have based your divorce petition on your spouse's adultery and have named the other person involved, that person is the co-respondent in the divorce suit and is entitled to be notified of the divorce proceedings. He or she will also receive a notice of proceedings and an acknowledgement of service and must return the completed acknowledgement of service to the court.

2. Where the respondent (and co-respondent) return the acknowledgement of service to the court indicating that they do not wish to defend the divorce – the special procedure

Very frequently, the respondent (and co-respondent if there is one) return the acknowledgement of service as instructed indicating that they do not intend to defend the divorce. The procedure that follows is quite straightforward:

a) The court will send your solicitor a copy of the completed acknowledgement of service together with copies of two more printed forms known as the 'request for directions for trial (special procedure)' and the 'affidavit of evidence (special procedure)'. The term 'special procedure' refers to the streamlined method by which a divorce can normally be obtained nowadays. Formerly, all petitioners seeking a divorce had to appear in open court and give evidence before a judge about their marriage and the reasons why they were claiming a divorce. This is no longer necessary in most cases because the court hearing has been replaced by written evidence confirming the details contained in the petition. Many people can now obtain a divorce without ever visiting court.

The affidavit of evidence – this is the document used to confirm that all the details given in your petition and the statement of arrangements are true, or in other words, the document that proves your case to the court. The affidavit is in questionnaire form and is designed to contain one or two more details about the matters you mentioned in your petition. Your solicitor will fill it in for you. He will ask you to have a look at the signature on the respondent's acknowledgement of service and confirm that this really is your spouse's signature – you will be required to state that this is so in the affidavit.

Your solicitor will give you the completed affidavit to read through – you must be very sure that the contents are accurate because you will then be asked to take an oath that everything in the affidavit is true. This procedure is called 'swearing' the affidavit. It is done either at the offices of another solicitor (on payment of a small fee) or at the court office (where no fee is payable). The fact that the affidavit has been sworn will be recorded at the end of it and it will be signed by the solicitor or court official in front of whom you took the oath. Whatever you say in your affidavit is just as much your evidence to the court as if you had stood in the witness box in the court room and stated the facts to a judge out loud.

The request for directions for trial – your solicitor will complete this very simple form requesting the court to proceed with your case.

The request for directions for trial and the affidavit of evidence are returned to the court by your solicitor. It is then up to the court to set in motion the next stage of the proceedings.

b) Once the request for directions for trial and the affidavit of evidence have been filed with the court, the next step is for the district judge to consider your case and decide whether he is satisfied that you have proved that you should be granted a divorce. You do not normally have to attend when the district judge considers your case but you will be notified, via your solicitor, of his decision.

If the district judge is happy with the case, he will give his certificate that you are entitled to a decree of divorce. If you have asked for the costs of the divorce to be paid by the respondent or co-respondent (see Chapter 4) the district judge will also consider this claim and anything that the respondent or co-respondent has had to say about it in the acknowledgement of service. If he is satisfied that you are entitled to the costs you claim, he will state this in his certificate.

If he is not satisfied about your claim to costs, he can refer the matter to the judge or district judge who will be pronouncing your decree nisi of divorce. The party who is objecting to your claim to costs will then be notified that he should attend at court on the day fixed for the pronouncement of the decree nisi to put his point of view to the judge/district judge. He may also be ordered to provide a written statement of his objections.

c) When the district judge has given his certificate that you are entitled to a divorce, a date will be fixed for decree nisi to be pronounced in open court by the judge or district judge. Although you and the respondent (and co-respondent) will be told when this is to take place, you do not need to attend unless there is any dispute over costs which has to be dealt with by the judge/district judge. If there is such a dispute both you and the party who is raising the objections to your claim should attend to explain the matter to the judge/district judge. This should rarely be necessary but, if it is, your solicitor will give you instructions as to what you should do and say.

d) You are free to go along to court to hear your decree nisi pronounced if you wish. If you decide to do so, you may be rather disappointed by the lack of ceremony involved – the whole procedure is likely to be over in a matter of minutes. The judge/district judge or a clerk of the court reads out or refers to a list of the names of the couples who are to be divorced that day – your name will be included in this list. The judge/district judge then announces that decree nisi of divorce is granted in each of the cases named. As soon as he has done this, you have completed the preliminary stage of the divorce by obtaining decree nisi.

e) Whether or not you decide to attend court for the pronouncement of decree nisi, you and the respondent (and co-respondent) will be sent a copy of the decree by the court. Your copy will probably reach you via your solicitor. You are *not* yet divorced – the decree nisi is simply a provisional decree of divorce and has to be converted into the final decree of divorce, or made 'absolute' at a later stage. It is only when decree absolute has been granted that your marriage is at an end and you are free to remarry (see Chapters 11 and 24).

f) *If the district judge is not satisfied that you are entitled to a divorce* when he considers your case, he can either give you the opportunity to produce further evidence in support of your case, or he can refer the whole case for a trial in open court to decide whether you should be granted a divorce. In this case, the special procedure will no longer be applicable and you will have to attend at court on a day which will be fixed for consideration of your case to give evidence personally of all the details contained in your petition. The court will then decide whether to grant your divorce. This procedure is not often needed these days.

If your case has to be dealt with in this way, you can apply for public funding to cover the cost of legal representation by your solicitor or a barrister at the hearing, provided, of course, you are eligible for public funding. If you are not, you will have to pay your solicitor to represent you but there may be some prospect of recovering your outlay, or some of it, from the respondent or co-respondent – your solicitor will advise you about this.

There is no need to worry about the hearing itself. It is normally quite brief and very straightforward, and your solicitor will tell you exactly what to do. You should not jump to the conclusion that, just because your case cannot be dealt with by the special procedure, this means that you will not get your divorce. Divorces are sometimes refused, but it is more likely that the court will be able to grant you a decree even though the district judge initially refused to give his certificate.

g) If, for any reason, you are refused a divorce, you should take your solicitor's advice as to whether there is any prospect of successfully renewing your application at a later date and as to the courses of action that are available meanwhile to help you resolve your difficulties despite the court's refusal to grant you a divorce (for example, you may wish to apply for a maintenance order, or for a sale of the family home to be ordered because you are in need of capital, or for questions relating to the children to be sorted out).

3. Where the respondent (or co-respondent) returns the acknowledgement of service to the court indicating that he intends to defend the case

If the respondent (or co-respondent) indicates in the acknowledgement of service that he wishes to defend the proceedings, your next step will depend on whether he files with the court a formal document called an 'answer' setting out his objections to your petition. He normally has 28 days after first receiving your divorce petition and the accompanying documents in which to file his answer with the court, although it is sometimes possible for a respondent or co-respondent who decides at a later stage that he wants to defend the case to file an answer even after this period has elapsed.

a) WHERE AN ANSWER IS FILED

If an answer is filed, the court will notify your solicitor and send him a copy of it. The special procedure can no longer be used. Unless the respondent (or co-respondent) changes his mind about defending the case, there will eventually be a hearing in open court at which you and the respondent (and the co-respondent) will be expected to attend and give oral evidence to a judge, who will consider whether, in the light of what you all have to say about the matter, a divorce should be granted. It is very rare for a divorce to reach this stage nowadays, however determined your spouse (or the co-respondent) may be to prevent the divorce being granted. No further details are therefore given in this book of the rather complicated procedures that are involved in a defended divorce. You, as the petitioner, would almost certainly be granted public funding to help with your legal costs of the defended divorce (provided your means are within the limits of the scheme). You would therefore be able to rely entirely on your solicitor to guide you through the proceedings. Unfortunately, you will usually find that, if the case is defended, quite considerable delays can be experienced in obtaining your divorce.

If you are a respondent (or co-respondent) and you are contemplating defending the proceedings, perhaps because you do not agree that your marriage has broken down irretrievably, or because you disagree with some of the things the petitioner has said in her petition, you are strongly advised to consult a solicitor before committing yourself in any way. Defending divorce proceedings can be a fruitless exercise that simply wastes the time and money of all concerned, without conferring any advantage on you. A solicitor will explain whether you have any prospect of defending the case successfully and what steps you can take, short of defending the divorce, if you disagree with any of the matters raised in the petition. If you do not wish to be divorced because you feel there is still a chance that you and your spouse could make a success of the marriage, you can talk over the question of a reconciliation with the solicitor, and he can raise the possibility of attempting a reconciliation with your spouse on your behalf.

If your solicitor feels that it would be worth your while to defend the petition, he will advise you how to go about this and whether you will be eligible for public funding to cover the legal costs involved (which can be substantial). However, it is only right to point out that it is very hard to obtain public funding to defend a divorce these days, however small your means.

b) WHERE NO ANSWER IS FILED

Not infrequently, the respondent (or co-respondent) indicates in the acknowledgement of service that he wishes to defend the case but then fails to file an answer within the 29 days allowed after he received the divorce papers. If this happens, the case will be dealt with by means of the special procedure as if the respondent (or co-respondent) has never intended to defend it. Your solicitor will be able to check with the court,

once the requisite period has elapsed, that it is in order to
proceed in this way. He will then obtain from the court the two
forms mentioned above, the affidavit of evidence and the
request for directions for trial. The procedure thereafter is
exactly the same as that described above in relation to a case
where the respondent (or co-respondent) has indicated in the
acknowledgement of service that he does not want to defend.

4. Where the respondent (or co-respondent) fails to return the acknowledgement of service

If the respondent (or co-respondent) does not return the
acknowledgement of service as required, proceedings will
usually be delayed whilst arrangements are made for someone
(often a court official called a court bailiff, or some other
independent person such as an enquiry agent) to visit the
respondent (or co-respondent) and make sure that he receives
copies of all the relevant papers. This procedure is known as
'effecting personal service' of the documents.

Once it is possible to satisfy the court that the respondent
(and co-respondent) have notice of the case, the normal
procedure can be put into operation to obtain the divorce
decree.

Sometimes it is impossible to trace the respondent to serve
him with the divorce papers, for example because you do not
know where he is living. Although difficulties of this kind can
give rise to delay, they are not normally insuperable. If
necessary, the court can be asked to make an order permitting
you to proceed with your petition even though you have been
unable to trace your spouse to inform him of the divorce
proceedings.

10

The Court Considers the
Arrangements for the Children

The procedure described in this chapter will only apply to families with children. If you have children, the following paragraph will tell you whether it applies to you.

1. The court's duty in relation to children

If you have children of the family (see Chapter 8) who are under 16, you will not normally be able to finalise your divorce by converting your decree nisi into decree absolute until the court has considered the arrangements you propose for these children and decided whether it needs to make any orders with regard to them, for example directing where the children should live, regulating contact with them or, where the court is particularly anxious about the children, requesting the social services to investigate their situation. If the court considers it necessary to do so, it will also assume a similar responsibility for children of 16 and over and review the arrangements you have made for them.

2. The respondent's views about the arrangements

You, as the petitioner, provide the court with details of the arrangements that you propose for the children when you complete and file with the court the statement of arrangements at the commencement of the divorce proceedings. The respondent receives a copy of this with your divorce petition and he may already have seen a copy when you tried to agree your proposals with him before filing the form in the first place.

If he agrees the arrangements, he should say so where indicated in the acknowledgement of service form that he will receive with the divorce papers. If he does not agree, he should indicate this on the form and also write promptly to the court setting out the matters he wants to raise. This letter should reach the court, if possible, within eight days after he receives the divorce papers and it must obviously reach the court before the district judge considers the arrangements for the children. It is particularly helpful for the respondent to inform the court of all he knows about the arrangements for the children if you and he have agreed between you that he is to look after the children on a permanent basis in the future rather than you.

If the respondent does write to the court commenting on the arrangements for the children, your solicitor will receive a copy of his letter from the court so that you are aware of his views.

3. The court considers the arrangements

Once he has decided that you are entitled to decree nisi, the district judge will consider the arrangements for the children. He does this in private and neither you nor the respondent will be invited to attend although he will obviously consider what you have said in the statement of arrangements and any views of which the respondent has notified the court.

Normally the district judge will decide after his initial consideration that there are no children of the family with whom he need concern himself (for example where your children are all aged 16 or over and have left school and are well able to fend for themselves) or, where there are relevant children, that the arrangements you have made for the children are satisfactory so that the court does not need to make any orders with regard to them. In either of these cases, he will give a certificate to this effect and both you and the respondent will be sent a copy. This will enable you to finalise your divorce in due course by applying to have your decree nisi made absolute.

If the district judge is not satisfied with the arrangements for the children, he has a number of options. He can, for example, ask you or the respondent to provide further written information about the arrangements or he can commission a welfare report on the children or fix a date for you and/or the respondent to come for a personal interview with him.

If you and the respondent are in dispute over the children and one or both of you is seeking an order in relation to them (for example, deciding where they are to live or arrangements for contact), consideration and/or approval of the arrangements may have to wait until the dispute is resolved, depending on the nature and extent of your disagreement.

Should the district judge not be able to give a certificate about the arrangements for the children or should you be involved in a dispute with your spouse about the children, your solicitor will assist you. He will advise you whether you can get public funding to cover the cost of him sorting things out for you and/or he may be able to give you advice and help under the Legal Help scheme if you are eligible for assistance under that scheme.

11

Obtaining Decree Absolute

Decree nisi is only a provisional decree of divorce. Your divorce becomes final when decree nisi is confirmed (made absolute) by the court.

When can decree nisi be made absolute?

There are several conditions that must be fulfilled before decree nisi can be made absolute:

a) Decree nisi cannot normally be made absolute until at least *six weeks* after the date on which the decree nisi was granted.

In very exceptional cases, it is possible for decree nisi to be made absolute before the six week period has elapsed. This is called 'expediting' the decree absolute and special permission is required from the court before it can be done. Permission is very rarely granted but if you feel there are good reasons why the court should permit you to finalise your divorce within a shorter period than normal, you should raise the matter with your solicitor as soon as possible (preferably even before your divorce petition is filed) so that he can advise you on your prospects of obtaining special permission and can make the necessary application to the court if he thinks it is worthwhile.

b) If you have children of the family whose welfare has to be considered by the court, you will not normally be allowed to apply for the decree to be made absolute until the district judge has considered the arrangements for them and granted his certificate indicating that the court need not take any further action with regard to them. You will find further details of the provisions relating to arrangements for your children in Chapter 10.

c) If you have obtained decree nisi of divorce on the basis of two years' separation and consent or five years' separation, the respondent can make a special application to the court under section 5 or section 10 of the Matrimonial Causes Act

1973 (MCA 1973) to have his or her financial position after divorce considered. If the respondent makes such an application in your case, you will not be allowed to have your decree made absolute until it has been dealt with. Do not confuse this type of application with the far more common application made by most spouses, requesting the court to sort out their finances and property after divorce for them (often known as an application for ancillary relief). The fact that you or your spouse has asked the court to make financial and property adjustment orders of this latter kind (dealt with in Chapter 20) will not prevent you from obtaining decree absolute, even if the questions you have raised have not yet been resolved.

(i) *Section 5 of the MCA 1973*: if you petition for divorce on the basis that you have been living separately from the respondent for five years, and you cannot prove any other fact, such as adultery, that would entitle you to a divorce (see Chapter 7), the respondent has a special right to oppose the divorce on the basis that, if it were granted, she (as most applications under sections 5 and 10 are made by wives, 'she' will be used, but the same principles apply to husbands) would suffer *grave financial or other hardship* and that it would be *wrong in all the circumstances to permit the divorce*. If the court supports her argument, it can refuse to grant you a divorce.

Before the new legislation on pensions, which gives the courts power to make pension sharing orders (see Chapter 20), section 5 of the MCA 1973 was in some cases the only way the courts could protect a respondent from losing her rights to a valuable widow's pension if the petitioner were to die first. Even then it was rare for a divorce to be refused on this basis, and no doubt since the new provisions on pensions have been introduced successful applications under section 5 will have become even more unusual.

The *other hardship* resulting from divorce referred to in section 5 is not defined, but has always been particularly difficult to establish. It might be argued that the respondent would become a social outcast in her community because of the prevailing social and religious attitudes to divorce, but it would not be enough that the divorce would cause her personal unhappiness or that she considers it morally wrong.

(ii) *Section 10 of the MCA 1973*: if you seek your divorce on the basis of two years' separation and consent, or on the basis of five years' separation, and you are unable to prove any other fact that would entitle you to a divorce, the respondent could hold up the making of the final decree of divorce (decree absolute) until the court has reviewed her financial position as it will be after the divorce and satisfied itself that either you should not be required to make financial provision for her, or the provision you have made is fair and reasonable or the best that can be made in the circumstances.

The court will consider all the circumstances of your case including your ages, health, earning capacity, financial resources and obligations. If for some reason (for example, so that you can remarry) you want to finalise the divorce, and intend and will formally undertake to make proper provision for the respondent but cannot do so straight away, the court does have the power to order decree absolute even though it is not yet satisfied with the financial provision made for the respondent.

Applications under sections 5 and 10 of the MCA 1973 can be complex: if such an application is likely in your case, it will be particularly important for you to consult a solicitor.

How to apply

The application to have decree nisi made absolute is very straightforward. It involves completing a simple form (obtainable from the court office) which is then returned to the court office dealing with your divorce. Once your form has been handed in, the district judge will check that all the conditions described above are fulfilled. If everything is in order, the district judge will grant decree absolute. You and the respondent will then be sent a copy of the official order. Keep it safely – it shows that your marriage has been finally dissolved. You may need to produce it to prove that you are divorced, for example if you wish to get married again in the future.

Do not leave it too long before applying for decree absolute
If you allow more than twelve months to pass between
obtaining decree nisi and applying for decree absolute, your
application must be accompanied by a written explanation for
the delay and you may be required to explain the delay in an
affidavit to the district judge. If you cannot satisfy him that
you have a reasonable explanation, he can refer the matter to a
judge and you will be required to explain to his satisfaction
before you are granted decree absolute.

Can a respondent apply for decree absolute?
If the petitioner does not apply for decree nisi to be made
absolute within three months of the time when she could first
have applied, the respondent is entitled to take the matter into
his own hands and apply for decree absolute himself. The
procedure is slightly less straightforward than when the application is made by the petitioner, because a short court hearing
in front of the district judge will be required instead of a
simple application form.

PART 3:
PERSONAL COMFORT AND SAFETY AND OCCUPATION OF THE HOME

12

Personal Protection and the Occupation of the House

If you are lucky, you and your spouse may be able to go your separate ways as soon as you realise that your marriage is at an end. Or you may, at least, manage to tolerate each other until the divorce is over and arrangements can be made to share out your property so that you can each find yourself somewhere to live.

But you may be less fortunate. You are both likely to be tense and emotional, perhaps even bitter, because your marriage is breaking down. You may start to get on each other's nerves and you may well have no choice but to live in the same house because neither of you is able (or willing) to find somewhere else to live. In this sort of situation, relations between you can become increasingly strained. You may never have thought that you and your spouse were capable of abusive behaviour or violence towards each other but you may find that you begin to torment and try to hurt each other, perhaps by taunting, or threats, or even with physical violence – anything from the occasional push or slap to more serious assaults.

Do you stay and put up with it? Or do you move out and tackle the problem of finding temporary accommodation? You already know the problems you are up against if you stay at home: if you move out there will be other issues to contend with – for example, where will you go? What will happen to the children if you take them with you? What will happen to them if you don't? How will you get to work and the children to school?

Some people are not even fortunate enough to have any choice in the matter – their spouse simply turns them out of the house against their will.

The courts are able to help considerably with all these sorts of problems, and this chapter outlines the type of thing the court can do to tide you over until matters improve.

What can the court do to help?
Alice's case is a good example of the help that the court can give.

Alice and Bill were married in 1994. They have three children. They were fairly happy when they were first married but things started to go wrong after their third child was born. Bill began to go out every night, leaving Alice to look after the children. He did not come in until late, and when he did return, he was often drunk. As relations between Alice and Bill got worse, he started to drink more and could not get up in the mornings. In the end he lost his job for bad time keeping and could not find another. From then on he began to spend his time at the pub and the betting shop and he never had any money to give Alice for housekeeping. He began to take things out on Alice; at first he just shouted at her and abused her, but some time ago he came in drunk one night and hit her about her face and body. From then on he was violent to her quite frequently. Once he pushed her over so that she hit her head against the cooker and had to have stitches for a cut on her forehead.

Alice was at the end of her tether and was frightened for herself and the children. She decided that she would have to move out of the house – Bill threatened that he would throw her out anyway if she did not go of her own accord. She took the children and went to her mother's. Her mother has not got a very big house and conditions with three children all under 10 years of age were overcrowded so they could not all go on living there very long. Her mother also lives in a different area which made it awkward for Alice to get to work and it took half an hour to get the children to school each morning.

Bill telephoned repeatedly, mostly in the middle of the night, to ask Alice to return. When she refused to do so, he threatened her and her mother. Alice saw him hanging around at the end of her mother's road on numerous occasions. She did not feel that she could go back to live in the same house as Bill with things as they were. Nor did she feel that she could cope with the situation as it was. She decided she would have to seek assistance from the court.

Alice needed two kinds of help. She needed somewhere suitable where she and the children could live, and she needed to be protected from Bill. The court was able to give her both sorts of assistance.

As Alice was looking after the children, it was obviously most practical if she lived in the family home with them. The only question was whether she could go back to live there with Bill if the court stepped in to prevent him from harming her and generally making a nuisance of himself, or whether Bill would have to leave so that Alice and the children could live in peace and safety. The court made an order preventing Bill from distressing Alice by using violence or threats or other abusive conduct towards her. It considered making a similar order preventing Bill from harming or tormenting the children, but decided that there was no real danger that he would do so. The court then considered the question of the house. It also decided that it was necessary to exclude Bill from the house completely so that Alice could go back to live there. Because Bill had hung around Alice's mother's house, the court additionally took the view that there was a danger that he would be inclined to come back to the matrimonial home and hang around upsetting and annoying Alice. It therefore made an order prohibiting him from coming within a specified distance of the house.

If Alice and Bill had had a fairly large house, there may have been a half way measure open to the court – it could have regulated what part of the house Bill should be allowed to use, leaving the rest of the house for Alice and the children. For example, if there had been five bedrooms and two bathrooms, the court could have ordered Bill to keep to one of the bedrooms and one bathroom. Together with an order prohibiting Bill from interfering with Alice in any way, this might have been enough to tide the family over until the divorce came through and their property could be sorted out so that they could each make arrangements for a home of their own. As it was, Bill moved out of the house within the time limit set by the court and went to live with his mother. Although he found it hard, he obeyed the court order and kept out of Alice's way completely so that he could not be tempted to annoy her or hurt her in any way. However, he was able to arrange to see the children every week.

How do I go about getting help from the court?

Help is available from either the family proceedings (magistrates') court or the county court. Your solicitor will advise you which court is appropriate for your case. Husbands and wives are equally entitled to be protected by the court, although it is more common for a wife to seek help. This chapter therefore assumes that it is the wife who is applying to the court; the same principles apply where a husband seeks help. In some cases, it may be appropriate for each of you to ask the court to intervene in some way. For example, you may each require protection against the conduct of the other. If the circumstances warrant it, there is no reason why the court should not deal with applications from both of you at the same time.

It is not necessary for either of you to have started divorce proceedings before you apply. Nor is it essential that you are still living together – some of the most acute problems are likely to arise when one of you has been expelled from the home by the other. Furthermore, it does not matter who owns the house, or in whose name a tenancy is.

If you need help, the first step is to consult your solicitor *without delay*. It will be far more difficult to convince the court that you really do need protection if you have left it for some time after the last incident before you try to do something about the situation. There are two types of order that can be made: a *non-molestation order* and an *occupation order*.

Non-molestation order

A non-molestation order is designed to offer personal protection against violent or abusive or other anti-social behaviour by your spouse towards you or the children. Alice's case provides an illustration of the type of conduct that can often justify such an order – actual violence, threats of violence, frequent and distressing abuse, repeatedly telephoning at unsocial hours, hanging around in an attempt to argue with and abuse the other spouse, etc. However, you should be careful not to cry wolf! You will be expected to put up with a fair amount of unpleasantness and irritation as a result of the breakdown of your marriage before the court will step in.

In deciding whether to make a non-molestation order, the court will look at all the circumstances of the case, including the need to secure the health, safety and well-being of you and any relevant child.

Occupation order

Using an occupation order the court can exclude your spouse from part or all of the family home and even from the area around it. It can also order him to permit you to return to live there if he has turned you out or is preventing you from entering.

In deciding whether to make such an order, the court will look at all the circumstances, including your financial situation and that of your spouse, the housing needs and resources of you, your spouse and your children, the likely effect of making or not making an order on the health, safety and well-being of all the members of the family and the conduct of you and your spouse. The question the judge must ask himself is whether your spouse's behaviour will cause you or a child of the family more harm if an order *is not* made than the harm caused to your spouse or a child of the family if the order *is* made. In other words, he will do a balancing exercise.

If you have children, the court will concentrate especially on how the situation is affecting them, in particular whether there is a risk of significant harm to one of them. It will want to know how much it is distressing the children to see the relationship between you and your husband deteriorate; what effect it would have on them if your husband was ordered to leave and how they would be affected if he was to stay; whether they are being directly involved in the breakdown of your marriage, perhaps because your spouse has threatened violence towards them or because you cannot help drawing them into arguments between you. The court will also need to know which of you is to look after the children – if you cannot make this decision yourselves, it may have to make a decision for you. The parent who is going to look after the children will frequently be allowed to stay in the house whilst the other spouse will have to move out.

When the court has all the information it needs, it is likely to approach its decision on the house in two stages. It will first decide whether the situation is so bad that you can no longer go on living together as a family in the same house. If it considers that this point has been reached, it then has to decide how things can be arranged so that you and your spouse do not come into contact with each other any more than is necessary.

If you have only got a small house, there may be no choice but to order one of you to move out. If you have more room, it may be possible for the court to divide up the house and allocate part to each of you so that you do not get under each other's feet. Either way, the court will have to decide who is to move out or who needs most space in the house.

If there is a serious possibility of your husband making a nuisance of himself in the vicinity of the house at any time after he has been ordered to leave, the court can be asked to make a further order prohibiting him from coming within a specified distance of the house, for example, he may be ordered not to come within 50 yards of the house, or to enter the road in which it is situated.

When making an occupation order, the court can also make an ancillary order regulating matters such as who is going to pay the rent or mortgage or be responsible for repairs.

As with a non-molestation order, an occupation order will only be used if you can satisfy the court that the situation in your home goes well beyond that of the normal disturbance and irritation that can be expected as part of a marriage breaking down. Because it involves forcing someone out of their home, an occupation order is regarded as a particularly drastic measure.

Will I have to attend court to get the order?
Yes, you will have to attend court to give evidence about your circumstances and you may also have to swear an affidavit setting out in writing the reasons why you need the court's help. Except in very urgent cases (for which, see ex parte orders below), the respondent will normally also have an opportunity to give evidence at the court hearing, and, if there is time before the hearing, may file an affidavit setting out his side of the story.

How long will the court's order last?
It is up to the court to decide how long its order should last. It may specify the period in the order (often three months and usually not more than six months in the first instance) or provide that it will remain in place until the court makes a further order in the case. The court will not make a further order unless you or your husband specifically ask at a later date that the order is altered or discharged.

When making an occupation order, the court also has the power to order that it should last until a particular event occurs. Generally because occupation orders are likely to cause greater inconvenience, they do not last for as long as non-molestation orders. They are not intended to resolve the question of your accommodation for good but to tide you over until you can make alternative arrangements or start divorce proceedings so that the court has an opportunity to deal with long term arrangements for your family property. If you are still in difficulties at the end of the order, it is usually possible to apply to the court to extend it.

If either of you wants the terms of an order varied or discharged completely, for instance because you have become reconciled since it was made, you are free to ask the court to make a further order.

Living together whilst the court's order is in force

If you obtain a non-molestation order against your spouse, this does not necessarily mean that you will be living separately; it simply regulates his conduct towards you. On the other hand, if you obtain an occupation order, this usually entails your spouse moving out of the house or at least living in a separate part of it. If you both want to give things another try and start living as a couple again, the court will not stand in your way but, depending on the precise terms of the occupation order, you or your spouse may need to apply to have the order discharged before you resume cohabitation. Your solicitor will advise you.

Seeing the children when the court order is in force

Provided your husband has not specifically been prevented by the court from seeing the children he will normally be entitled to do so even though a non-molestation order is in force or he has been excluded from the home. However, you may have to be prepared to alter your arrangements over contact to make sure that they do not involve your husband in breaching the court's order. For example, if your husband has been ordered not to come within 50 yards of the house, he will not be able to pick the children up at the door and you may have to arrange for a neighbour or relative to take them to the end of the road to meet him.

How quickly can I get an order?

The court will not normally deal with your application until your spouse has been notified of it and given a chance to attend at court to put his side of the story. However, the court has power to make an *ex parte* order (an order made on your application alone without your spouse being informed) if it considers that it would be just and convenient to do so. In deciding whether to proceed in this way, the court will consider:

- whether the urgency of the situation requires an order to be made immediately because of the harm you or a child may suffer from your spouse's conduct otherwise
- whether you are likely to be put off or prevented from coming to court again for help if you fail to get an order right away, and
- whether there is reason to believe that your husband is deliberately avoiding being given notice of the proceedings by making himself impossible to find and that you or your children will be seriously prejudiced by the delay involved.

The same criteria apply whether you are applying for an ex parte non-molestation order or an ex parte occupation order. However, as an occupation order excluding someone from his home is a particularly drastic measure, it is likely that the court will be very reluctant to make an occupation order without first giving your spouse a chance to have his say.

If an ex parte order is made, it will last for only a very short time (usually a week), just sufficient to tide you over until a hearing can be arranged at which both of you can explain your positions fully to the court.

The time actually taken to obtain an order, either in an emergency or in the normal way, will depend on all the circumstances – it will depend not only on the complexity of your case but also on how busy the court is. It is sometimes possible to consult your solicitor in the morning and to have obtained a court order by the end of the day. On the other hand, if you are applying by routine procedure, it may take a week, or, in some cases, considerably more time before you have your order.

If you are really frightened of what your spouse might do, make this clear to your solicitor – he does not necessarily know your spouse personally and, unless you tell him, he may not appreciate how much you need the court's protection.

Undertakings to the court

It may be possible for your spouse to make a promise to the court about his behaviour or the occupation of the home instead of the court having to make an order regulating things. Such a promise to the court is called an 'undertaking' and it is just as effective as a court order: if your husband breaks the promise, he is liable to exactly the same penalties as if he had broken the terms of an order. The only disadvantage is that you cannot obtain a power of arrest (see below) with an undertaking, only with a court order.

Enforcing the court's order

In many cases, the fact that the court has made an order will be enough to resolve the situation between you and your husband because he will comply with whatever the court decides. However, things are not quite so simple if your husband fails to obey the order, for instance if he does not move out of the house as he was ordered to do or he continues to use violence towards you or to harass you in some other way.

Your next step depends on whether you were granted a *power of arrest* with the court order. This is a special order entitling the police to arrest your spouse straight away if they have reasonable cause to suspect that he is in breach of the court order. Where your spouse has used or threatened violence against you or one of the children, the court is required to attach a power of arrest to any occupation or non-molestation order unless it is satisfied that you or the child will be adequately protected without it. The power of arrest can last for as long as the order but will often last for three months even if the order lasts longer. If a power of arrest is still necessary at the end of that period, you will be able to apply to the court to extend it.

If a power of arrest is granted with your order, and your husband breaches the court's order, you should contact your local police station. A police constable can then arrest your husband at once. If this happens he will be taken into custody and brought before the court within 24 hours.

Contact your solicitor as soon as possible after the incident so that he is aware of what is happening and can look after your interests. It is the responsibility of the police to arrange for your husband to be taken to court, but you will almost certainly have to give evidence to the judge or magistrates about what happened.

The court will have to decide what should be done about your husband's conduct. It can send him immediately to prison for whatever period it thinks appropriate. This is less likely to happen if it is the first time he has broken the court order, as imprisonment is usually reserved as something of a last resort for people who have persistently disobeyed the court's orders. Alternatively, the court can give your husband a suspended sentence of imprisonment, phrased so that if he breaks the court order again within a particular period of time, often three or six months, then he will be imprisoned. The court can also fine your husband.

There are often other, more constructive, courses of action open to the court instead of imprisonment. The court may decide to modify its original order in the light of what has happened. For instance, suppose that your husband has failed to comply with an order prohibiting him from molesting you because he simply cannot keep his temper when he is in contact with you – the court could, in these circumstances, modify its original order to exclude your husband from the home so that you have no further contact with each other. Another alternative would be to put off the hearing for some time to give your husband one more chance to comply with the original order.

If you are not granted a power of arrest, it is up to you, with your solicitor's help, to take steps to bring your husband back to court if he breaks the order so that the court can decide what is to be done. You may, for example, be able to apply to court for a warrant to be issued for your spouse to be arrested for failing to abide by the court's order. In order to obtain this, you will have to make a statement sworn on oath about the ways in which he has broken the order. Once you have brought the matter back before the court, the court has the same powers over your husband as it does where he is brought before it by means of a power of arrest.

The proceedings described so far in this chapter are 'civil' proceedings, in other words, they do not involve a criminal prosecution. However, if your spouse assaults you or damages your property, or persistently harasses you, for example by 'stalking' you, he will have committed a criminal offence just as he would if he behaved in this way to any other person.

If something of this kind occurs you can call the police even if you do not have a power of arrest with your order, although you may find that they are reluctant to interfere without the backing of a power of arrest. Nevertheless, they may be prepared to come out to the incident and try to calm things down. They may sometimes even take criminal proceedings against your spouse depending on the particular circumstances of your case.

If you are dissatisfied that the police are not prosecuting your husband, you may be able to bring a criminal prosecution against him yourself. This could result in his being sentenced to imprisonment. However, this course of action really only deals with what is past, and gives you no guarantee that you will be protected in the future. Furthermore, you would be expected to meet the cost of the case out of your own pocket, whereas with civil proceedings you may well be eligible for public funding (formerly known as legal aid).

Does the court's order affect your own or your spouse's rights to your house?

Orders excluding your spouse from the home have no effect on the question of who owns the house. If your husband is the owner of the house but is ordered to leave for a period of time, he still owns the property even though he is temporarily prevented from enjoying the rights that an owner normally has.

The question of who should own and live in the house in the long term will be dealt with when the court considers what should be done about your property and finances in the long term, after the divorce.

Paying for your application
If you are financially eligible, you can get public funding under the Legal Help Scheme for legal advice about non-molestation or occupation orders, or for making applications for such orders.

PART 4:
THE CHILDREN

13
The Children: Introduction

There is no escaping the fact that even the most straightforward divorce will have some effect on your children. It inevitably brings with it a complete change in lifestyle for the whole family to which it will take some time for you all to grow accustomed. Children are often very conservative by nature and can find it particularly difficult to accept that family life, as they used to know it, has now gone for good. At times you may be tempted to wish that you had stayed together for the sake of the children and never embarked on a divorce at all. Nevertheless, if your marriage has completely broken down, divorce is often the most sensible solution, and, if you find the whole process rather discouraging at times, you should bear in mind that the children may have been caused a great deal more distress in the long run if you had gone on living together in a state of constant friction.

Once you have decided on divorce, the best you can do for the children is to try to make the process as painless as possible for them. This chapter attempts to give you some idea of how problems that arise in relation to the children can be resolved. Every family reacts differently to stress and no one can warn you of all the difficulties with which you may have to cope. Nevertheless, there are some problems that seem to crop up over and over again and, as well as explaining the legal side of things, this chapter and the following two chapters try to offer some general advice to help you overcome or avoid difficulties that may arise.

Nothing that is suggested as general advice is in any way an 'expert opinion' on how to help children to cope with divorce

– it is simply a mixture of the conclusions drawn from meeting
families involved in divorce proceedings and common sense.
Though sometimes it may seem like the counsel of perfection,
if you bear the advice in mind, we hope you may at least find
that it helps you to deal with the situations with which you are
faced.

If you experience serious difficulties with your children
(other than of a legal nature) you are urged to seek expert help
from those qualified to deal with such problems. You should
be able to find out who would be most suitable by discussing
the matter with your doctor or the child's teacher. With
children of school age, it is usually a good idea to keep in
contact with the child's school anyway and to ask his teacher
to tell you if he shows any signs at school of being disturbed
over the divorce. You may also find it useful to contact an
organisation that offers help and moral support with your
predicament. Chapter 26 gives some suggestions as to how to
get in touch.

THE LEGAL FRAMEWORK

Do not assume that just because you are getting divorced, you
will need a court order in relation to your children. The old
practice of the courts was to make orders regulating where
the children were to live (custody orders) and what contact
there was to be (access orders) as a matter of course in every
divorce case. The Children Act 1989 has introduced a completely new approach, however, and provides that an order
should only be made where this would be better for the child
than making no order at all. So, where the parents are able to
agree upon what the arrangements will be for the children
after the divorce, the court will simply check that those
arrangements are satisfactory in accordance with its duty in
the divorce proceedings (see Chapter 10) and then leave it up
to the parents to act in accordance with their agreement
without a court order. Only if there is a dispute, will the court
need to intervene and make an order under the Children Act
1989.

Should you need to seek assistance from the courts, section

8 of the Children Act 1989 provides a range of orders which can be used to resolve issues in relation to children. Custody and access orders have now been replaced by four main types of order:

a) a *residence order* which settles the arrangements as to where a child is to live (normally this will be with one of his parents though third parties such as uncles, aunts and grandparents can sometimes apply for residence orders as well);

b) a *contact order* which regulates the contact that a child has with the person named in the order (normally the absent parent though third parties such as other relatives can obtain contact orders too);

c) a *prohibited steps order* which prohibits a parent from exercising his parental responsibility for a child in whatever way is stipulated in the order, for example a parent could be prohibited from arranging for the child to become a member of an extreme religious faith;

d) a *specific issue order* which decides a particular question that has arisen or may arise in connection with any aspect of parental responsibility for a child, for example where the child should be educated.

The court has power to make an order whenever one is necessary, whether or not divorce proceedings have been commenced. If a divorce petition has been filed with the court or divorce proceedings are planned, the county court will almost certainly deal with the application. In other situations, an application may be made to the magistrates' court instead.

GENERAL ADVICE

1. Keeping a united front

In the course of the divorce you will have to make a large number of decisions with your spouse over the future of the children. They will range from the most major decision – where the child is going to live when you separate – to decisions over contact arrangements, education and religion, etc.

However much you may fight over each decision in private, you should do your utmost not to let the children become aware of this. Even very young children sense surprisingly quickly that there is a dispute going on between their parents over their future and they often find it very distressing. It is generally easier for children to accept decisions made for them if they feel that both parents are in agreement. If they sense a serious difference of opinion, they may start taking sides, or may feel very reluctant to accept what has been decided for fear of hurting the parent who did not fully agree with the decision.

If there has to be a court hearing over any questions relating to the children, it will be almost impossible to hide your differences of opinion from the children. It is far better for all concerned, therefore, if you can reach agreement over all the decisions you have to make jointly and thus avoid the need for a court to investigate and impose its judgments on the whole family.

2. The importance of giving careful thought to every decision that you make

Every decision that you make about the lives of your children is worthy of very careful consideration. It is easy, when you are feeling the strain of divorce, to make rash and emotional decisions which you will later come to regret. So, before you come to any final conclusions on a problem, make sure that you have truly found the solution that is *best for your child*, even if it is not necessarily what you feel will bring you the most happiness.

If you feel that the children should know what is going on and what decisions have been made on their behalf, it will help them if you make sure that you can explain the situation to them in a way that they will understand and be able to accept, so it is often a good idea to sit down quietly first and consider how you are going to approach a particular matter with them.

Before you involve any of the children in any of the actual decision making, you should be absolutely sure that it is right for the particular child to be brought into discussions in this way. Whereas older children may have very clear views about a matter that they would welcome an opportunity to make known, younger children may be upset if you ask them what their feelings are but then their wishes have to be overruled.

3. Your attitude to the other parent

It is very tempting, when you are going through the process of a divorce, often feeling lonely and vulnerable, to try to get all your friends and relations on your side. Many people under-standably also become anxious about losing the affection of their child to the other parent and, in an attempt to prevent this, sometimes start to run down the other parent in front of the child and try to discourage the child from seeing him or her.

Once you are divorced and you are hoping to make a fresh start in life, your first reaction may well be to sever all your connections with your former spouse. However, if the children are to go on seeing him or her you will not be able to cut yourself off completely and you may find that you resent this.

It is only in very exceptional circumstances that the court will permit a clean break between the children and their other parent to take place, if that parent wants to go on seeing the children. You will make life much easier and happier for yourself and the children if you encourage contact between the children and their other parent and take great care not to try to turn the children against him or her and to keep any bad feelings that you may have about the whole subject strictly to yourself. You will probably find that as the children grow older, they will be very grateful to you for maintaining as normal a relationship with the other parent for them as is possible in the circumstances, whereas children who have been discouraged from seeing their other parent may grow up to resent this and sometimes even turn against the parent responsible.

4. Coping with a reaction against you

When one parent looks after the day to day needs of the child and the other parent only sees the child for short periods, the other parent naturally wants (and can often afford) to give the child treats and to spoil him when he sees him, whereas the parent with full time responsibility for the child has to maintain standards, keep within a tight budget and be responsible for discipline where necessary. Children do not always realise the reason why it may seem to be so much fun to be with the other parent. As a result, they sometimes make hurtful remarks to the parent who is responsible for their day to day care. There is no easy way round this and if you are the parent who has the privilege of the full time care of the child you may find that you have to put up with attempts by the child to play one parent off against the other, or with comments from the child such as 'I want to live with Daddy because he gives me sweets/takes me for a ride in his car/lets me play in the park . . .' or 'I'll tell Dad if you don't let me do such and such and he will let me go to live with him'. Behaviour of this kind, although it can be very upsetting for you, often does not mean very much; it is certainly very unlikely to mean that the child really does not want to go on living with you any more.

As the 'other parent' you can, of course, ease the situation by trying not to spoil the child when you see him, however tempting it might be, and making an effort not to say anything in front of the child that may undermine your ex-spouse's authority.

5. Publications and organisations which may help

The Department of Constitutional Affairs (see Chapter 26 for contact details) produces some helpful pamphlets about parenting in a divorce situation such as 'Parenting Plan', which helps you plan for your children's future, 'My Family's Splitting Up' and 'Parents and Children'. *One Parent Families* (see Chapter 26) also publish a number of helpful leaflets including a booklist of books for you to read to younger children and books to give to older children which may help them to cope with your divorce. A few examples of such books are given at the end of Chapter 26.

14
The Children:
Residence Orders and Other Issues

If you and your spouse are in dispute as to where the children should live, it will pay to make use of the mediation service or negotiate through solicitors if you can to resolve your differences. Fighting bitter court battles will make it more difficult to establish a reasonable parenting relationship with the other parent in future and it is likely that the people you will hurt most are your children. However, if you cannot come to an agreement about this issue, you will need to go to court to obtain a residence order. Whatever the residence order decides about living arrangements, however, you will both continue to have parental responsibility for the children. Obviously, the parent with whom a child is living will have to make the routine day to day decisions for the child (what time the child should go to bed, whether homework comes before television, what time an older child must be in at night, etc.) but the other parent is entitled to participate in more major decisions over matters such as education, religion, etc. If the absent parent has strong views about important issues such as these and agreement cannot be reached between the parties, one or other parent can seek a specific issue order or a prohibited steps order (see Chapter 13) and the court will decide. Do note particularly that where there is a residence order in force with regard to a child, there are certain automatic restrictions on the freedom of the child's parents to bring up that child as they choose. These are dealt with at the end of this chapter.

Residence orders can take various forms. The most common type of arrangement is for the children to live with one parent and to see the other parent at regular intervals for contact. In this situation there is a straightforward residence order in favour of one parent and a contact order in favour of the other. Despite the fact that more and more fathers are becoming actively involved in the care of their children these days, the most usual situation is still for the mother to be the parent with residence and the father to have contact so, when dealing with matters arising after a residence order, this chapter is written as if the court had ordered that the children reside with their mother. The same principles would, however, apply if arrangements were the other way round.

A residence order can be made in favour of more than one person where the circumstances merit it. This would enable the court, in an appropriate case, to grant a residence order to a mother and her new husband, for example, or, where the children spend roughly half their time with one parent and half with the other, there could be a split residence order stipulating which part of the week/year the children are to spend with their mother and which part with their father.

Although the Children Act 1989 has ensured that the courts will do their best to resolve any dispute that you may have over residence without delay, it can still be some time before you get a decision. Should you come up against problems in the meantime, the court has power to make a temporary order to tide you over. This is sometimes referred to as an 'interim residence order'. You might need to apply in this way, for example, if the other parent is looking after the children and will not agree to you taking over and you are seriously worried about the standard of care they are receiving. However in most cases you will find that, unless it is absolutely necessary to do so, the judge will be very reluctant to interfere with the existing arrangements until he has all the relevant information and is in a position to make a long term decision. (Throughout this chapter for ease of reference the district judge will be referred to as 'he' rather than 'he/she', although obviously the judge could be a man or a woman.) Your solicitor can advise on whether you should apply to the court for an interim order or simply press on with your application for a full residence order as quickly as possible.

If you are in dispute over the children, it is important to take legal advice straight away. Children soon settle into a home and a routine and the longer they spend with one parent, the less likely the court is to alter the arrangement and grant residence to the other parent, however good the package of care that he proposes.

Applying for an order

An application for a residence order is launched by filing a special form with the court – either form C1 or C2 depending on whether divorce proceedings have begun. These forms can be obtained from the court, along with leaflets to help you fill them in. On the form you will need to set out details with regard to the children, yourself, etc., and briefly summarise what orders you want the court to make and why. The application form is then served on the other parent who must then file with the court and serve on you an acknowledgement of the application.

Directions or conciliation appointment

Once the court has received your application, it will fix a directions appointment or conciliation appointment. A district judge will see you and your spouse, and your solicitors, in his private room. A court welfare officer (a social worker who is experienced in dealing with cases concerning children) will be there and you and your spouse will be expected to talk to him/her, to try and reach an agreement about arrangements for the children.

If you are able to agree, all the better for you and for your children. You may only be able to agree a short term arrangement, in which case the judge can set a date in, say, three or six months' time on which you can all attend court again if you need to.

If you cannot agree, the judge will decide whether any short term (interim) orders should be made to tide you over until the court can have a final hearing to decide the case. He will give directions as to how the matter is to proceed and will require both parents to file statements setting out their case. He will also ask for an independent report about your case to assist him with his decision. This report will be prepared by a 'children and family reporter' (a different court welfare officer from the one you saw at the directions appointment; for ease of reference this person will be referred to as 'he' rather than 'he/she'). He will normally want to discuss with each parent individually the family history, the proposals you are making for the children, and any worries that you have about the care the other parent would provide for the children if they were to live with him or her. He will also want to meet anyone else who is going to be in close contact with the children and make other enquiries, such as speaking to the child's teacher at school. Most children and family reporters like to meet all but the youngest children concerned in the case. It frequently helps them to see the children both in your company and on their own. They are very careful not to question the children directly about where they are to live unless they are obviously old enough to have clear views about it.

Once the children and family reporter has collected all the information he requires, he will prepare a written report for the court which will include information about your case and sometimes a recommendation, to which the judge will attach considerable weight, even if he does not follow it. You are entitled to see the report and it will either be sent to you directly or through your solicitor.

The court hearing

When all the evidence is ready, the next step is the hearing itself which will take place in front of the judge. The hearing is held in chambers, in private, and will be fairly informal. Only people who are directly concerned with the case will be allowed to be present – no members of the general public will be admitted. You may be asked to attend court earlier than the time fixed for the hearing so that you have time to discuss everything with your solicitor or barrister.

When the judge is ready to hear your case, either your solicitor (or barrister) or your spouse's will explain to the judge what the case is all about. Then either you or your spouse will give evidence first (on oath or having affirmed the truth of what you will say). When you give evidence you will be asked questions about the case to make sure that you cover all the matters about which the judge needs to know.

Any witnesses who have attended court may be given the opportunity to give their evidence during the proceedings and the children and family reporter will sometimes be called upon to give evidence also.

When all the evidence has been put before the court, the solicitors (or barristers) will have the opportunity to address the judge in support of your respective applications. The judge will then make his decision. Once you know the outcome of the case, it is always a good idea to have a word with your solicitor before leaving court. There are often matters arising from the decision to be sorted out, for example contact arrangements.

Later changes in the residence order
The order that the court makes after a full consideration of the evidence is usually designed to be a long term arrangement. However a residence order is never absolutely final and can always be altered if circumstances should change to make this necessary. This does not mean that a parent who is dissatisfied with the court's order can simply return to court a month later and ask for the decision to be changed. But it does mean that if, in the future, the parent who does not have residence has any serious worries about the way in which the children are being brought up, he has the right to re-open the whole question.

There are numerous reasons why the court might be prepared to alter the existing residence order, for example, if the parent who has residence is wrongly preventing the other parent from seeing the children, or if he or she has become unsuitable to care for the children since the original court hearing. There may also be more straightforward reasons for varying the original order, for example, the child may have expressed a firm wish to live with the other parent and both parents may agree that this wish should be respected.

It is extremely difficult to persuade the court to alter an existing residence order, unless both parties agree that this should be done. Judges generally feel that once a child has settled into a routine with one parent, there has to be a very strong reason to justify putting the child through all the upheaval that a variation of the residence order would cause.

How does a court decide where a child is to live?

When it makes its decision as to where a child is to live, the court is always guided by the same principle – that the child's welfare should come first.

No two cases will ever be the same so there can be no hard and fast rules about when a mother should have residence and when the father has the better claim. All the circumstances of the case will be considered by the judge before he makes his decision. You will have to turn to your solicitor for advice on the probable outcome of your own case, but you may find it helpful to know what sort of factors the judge will be likely to bear in mind when resolving an issue over residence.

(a) *The physical well-being of the child*
Most families nowadays are able to provide housing for their children, and state benefits generally ensure that provision can be made for the children's basic needs of food and clothing. The court will compare the standard of accommodation offered by each parent and assess how suitable it is for the child. For example, the judge might have to decide whether it would be better for a child to live with its mother in a high-rise flat in the centre of a big town or with its father in a detached house with a garden in the suburbs. At first sight the answer may seem to be obvious, but in fact, although it will be taken into consideration, the greater material prosperity and pleasanter surroundings offered by one parent will not normally be the decisive factor in a case. In any event, the courts are often able to go some way towards equalising the differences between the parents in this respect when they deal with the family property and maintenance after the divorce.

What is likely to be more important is the day to day care that each parent is likely to provide for the child. The judge will need to be sure that the child will be fed properly, that the home will be kept clean, that adequate clothing will be

provided and that suitable babysitting arrangements will
always be made for the child who is young enough still to
require this. If there is any serious doubt as to whether one of
the parents will live up to the required standards, that parent
will be at a disadvantage in the residence proceedings. If the
evidence suggests that a parent will actually neglect or ill treat
the child in some way, that parent will be very unlikely to get
a residence order.

Fortunately, in most disputes over residence, it is quite clear
that both parents will provide first class care for the child and
the court has no need even to consider this aspect of the case.

(b) *The special problems faced by the working parent*
For the parent who goes out to work, there will be a special
problem of who is to look after the children when he or she
cannot be there. Many couples nowadays both work, even
after they have a family. Both would have to find a substitute
to look after the children after school, or if they are ill, or in
school holidays, etc. The court will need to have details of the
outside help that each parent proposes to use. The court will
normally be more inclined to give residence to a parent who
will be relying on someone the children know and like, than to
a parent who has to rely on a total stranger.

Sometimes the court is faced with a situation where only
one of the parents (usually the father) goes out to work,
whereas the other can be at home full time to look after the
children. In such a case, of course, only the father will have to
rely on outside help with the children and he is bound to be at
a disadvantage in applying for residence because (where both
parents are equally suitable in all other respects) the court will
obviously be more inclined to grant residence to the mother
who can be there whenever the children need her.

(c) *Mother or father?*
In principle, neither parent has a better right to residence than
the other; it all depends on the circumstances of the case.
However, where the mother has been the full-time carer, she
will have the advantage. Also, there is a bias in favour of

mothers where the children are very young, but this becomes less strong as they get older.

(d) *The behaviour of both parents*
The court will not be prepared to investigate who has caused the breakdown of the marriage and how one parent has behaved towards the other, unless this behaviour has affected the children in some way or is likely to make the 'guilty' party unsuitable to look after them in the future. It is generally accepted that when a marriage is breaking down, there is inevitably a certain amount of unpleasant behaviour on the part of both spouses, which will not usually affect their capacity to be very good parents. On the other hand, there are cases where a parent has behaved in a way that does directly affect his or her suitability as a parent.

Perhaps an example will most easily help you to appreciate how the courts approach the matter. Let us suppose that Mrs A falls for Mr B during her marriage to Mr A. She continues to take perfectly good care of her children but, from time to time, she sees Mr B whilst the children are at school and has sexual intercourse with him. This fact alone does not make her unsuitable to be a mother in any way. But, suppose that after the divorce, she starts to go out at night, five or six times a week, leaving the children in the care of young babysitters. Each week or so she brings home a different boyfriend who sleeps with her in her bed. Behaviour of this kind may have a serious effect on the children and would affect Mrs A's suitability as a parent. Whereas the court would not wish to hear any evidence in the residence dispute about Mrs A's association with Mr B, it might well consider evidence of the second kind, of irresponsible behaviour, vital to its decision.

In another example, as their marriage deteriorates, Mr and Mrs C start to have frequent arguments. On one or two occasions, in the course of particularly heated arguments, Mr C loses his temper and slaps Mrs C across the face. She is not injured. The children are asleep in bed at the time and do not know anything about this. This lapse on the part of Mr C would not be likely to influence the court's decision in any way. On the other hand, if Mr C had been repeatedly violent towards his wife during the marriage, and had even beaten her up seriously in front of the children several times, this would weigh heavily against him in a residence dispute.

It is not only the behaviour of the parents towards each other that can be important. There are other aspects of the behaviour of a spouse that would be likely to have a bearing on the court's decision. For example, it may be very important for the court to know that one spouse is involved in prostitution, or has an unending criminal record, or a recurrent history of serious mental illness, or belongs to an extreme religious sect.

(c) *The family ties*
In some families there is a particularly strong bond between a child and one of his parents. The court will take this into account in deciding where the child is to live. Even if the child does not show any particular attachment to either parent, the court will need to be sure that the parent who gets residence will provide the child with the love, understanding, discipline and moral support that he will need as he grows up.

There is usually a close relationship between brothers and sisters, and the court is extremely reluctant to split them up between parents, although if there are very special circumstances that really justify such a course, the court can order that some of the children go to the mother and some to the father.

(f) *The need for stability in the child's life*
Children do not normally react well to change. Their lives are inevitably disrupted once when the marriage breaks down, and judges are very anxious to make sure that once they have started to get over this, they are subjected to as little change as possible in their daily lives. This means that the parent who has the day to day care of the children at the time when the residence application is heard will have a

considerable advantage over the other parent, particularly if the children have become settled with him or her for any length of time. If it would be right to move the child, the court will do so, but it will need to be given strong reasons why this is necessary.

(g) *The child's own view*
The judge is most likely to get to know the child's wishes regarding where he or she is to live (if he has expressed any) from the welfare report; much more infrequently, he will talk to the child himself. The older the child becomes, the more difficult it is to force him to accept a decision about residence with which he does not agree. So, if older children have clear views about where they would like to live, this will be a factor that will probably influence the judge's decision quite heavily. On the other hand the judge will always bear in mind that a child of any age may have been influenced by one of his parents or may not be voicing his true feelings for some other reason. The younger the child is, the less attention the court will pay to his own wishes about residence.

(h) *The attitude of each parent towards the other*
It is considered very important, in most cases, that the child should continue to have a good relationship with the parent with whom he does not live and to see that parent regularly. It will count against a parent if he or she attempts to spoil this relationship in any way, for example by making derogatory remarks about the other parent in front of the child or discouraging or preventing contact visits. In extreme cases, if a parent behaves particularly badly in this respect, it can be the deciding factor in the residence case.

(i) *The welfare report*
The welfare report is very important. If the children and family reporter makes a recommendation in respect of residence, this will carry a great deal of weight, although it is not the last word on the matter – that rests with the judge.

Some points to watch out for after the residence order

(a) *Changing your child's surname*
If you remarry after your divorce or revert to your maiden
name, you may want the children whom you look after to be
known by your new surname to save embarrassment and
inconvenience. However, the law provides that where a residence order is in force, no person shall cause the child to be
known by a new surname without the consent of everyone
with parental responsibility (in most cases this means both
parents) or the leave of the court. This provision prevents not
only a change of name by deed poll but also a less formal
arrangement whereby, for example, the child's school simply
changes his name on the register and calls him by a new
surname in class. If the other parent will not consent and you
have to apply to the court for permission, you will have to
convince the court that it is in the child's best interests to be
known by a new surname.

(b) *Taking the child abroad*
When a residence order is in force with respect to a child, with
one exception, no one may remove the child from the United
Kingdom without the written consent of every person with
parental responsibility (this usually means both parents) or
leave of the court. The only exception to this is that the person
in whose favour the residence order has been made can
remove the child temporarily for a period of less than a month.
If you are the parent with residence, you do not therefore need
to seek permission to go on holiday abroad.

This restriction is designed to prevent the sort of problem
about which you may have read in the newspapers where
one parent abducts the child, takes him or her abroad
without the knowledge of the other parent and then refuses
to bring him back. Once the child has left the United
Kingdom, the authorities in this country are very limited in
what they can do to assist in getting the child returned so, if
you genuinely fear that the other parent may intend to abduct
your child, you should contact your solicitor and the police

at once so that they can act to prevent him.

Whenever it considers an application to take a child abroad, whether temporarily or permanently, the court puts the welfare of the child first when making its decision. The court views it as a serious step to emigrate permanently with a child because it usually means that contact with the other parent is restricted or may have to cease altogether and it also means that the English courts no longer have effective control over the child's upbringing. Permission is not therefore granted automatically though the court will bear in mind that if it restricts your own freedom by thwarting your plans this may cause you to become resentful and bitter which, in turn, may affect the way in which you bring up your child so that it is not always in the child's best interests to refuse leave. If you are given leave by the court to remove a child from the United Kingdom, you may be required to undertake (promise) to the court to return him to this country at the end of your holiday or, if you are emigrating permanently, to return him should it ever become necessary to do so.

15
Seeing Your Child

If your child is not living with you, you are entitled to expect reasonable contact with him or her. What is reasonable varies according to the circumstances of your case – contact visits can range from long periods (perhaps even the whole of the school holidays) staying with the other parent, to an hour or two with him in the park.

The court will expect you to be able to agree over what contact is reasonable in your case. If you cannot do so, the court will decide the matter for you by defining when contact should take place. However, although this service is available, it is essential that you try to sort out as many of the arrangements as possible between yourselves and try to remain amicable over contact. If you do, you will make things so much easier for your children. Remember that although you have fallen out with each other, the children are probably still very much attached to each of you and it is most important for them to maintain contact with both of you. A contact visit can seem quite artificial and strained enough to a child without its being preceded by endless arguments between his parents.

Some parents, after they are divorced, are mistakenly tempted to try to cut off all contact between the child and the other parent. This happens for a variety of reasons. Frequently a mother will convince herself that this is the right thing to do because the father is a bad influence and upsets the child. However, the underlying reason may often be that she wants to make quite sure that she does not lose the child's love and affection to the other parent. What is more, she may still be feeling very hurt after the divorce and by preventing contact she may have one way in which she can hit back at her ex-husband.

It is only in quite exceptional cases, where there is strong evidence that it is not in the child's best interests to continue with contact, that contact will be prevented by the court when you want it to continue and are prepared to make efforts to see your child.

It may help to bear in mind the following points when deciding what contact you think is reasonable in your case:

1. If you left it up to the court to decide what contact should take place, the court would order whatever it thought was best for your child – you should use the same yardstick when agreeing your own arrangements.

2. Children who live with one parent and have contact with the other inevitably have to divide their time between two separate lives. As they grow older, they will make friends in the area where they live and will no doubt want to participate in all sorts of activities, usually at weekends, such as sports matches and school outings. It can be disappointing for them and cause resentment if they always miss this type of activity because contact visits have to take place on the day concerned. When fixing your contact arrangements you should take this into account; for example, it may not be a good idea to arrange for your child to spend *every* weekend with you because this will prevent him from having a normal home life – it would probably be better for him to stay with you every other weekend, or perhaps three weekends out of four.

As well as making sure that your child does not miss too many things he would like to do with his friends, wise parents remain flexible about contact for other reasons. It is in the interests of both of you to do so as you will probably each want to take advantage of the flexibility of arrangements from time to time.

If your child tells you he wants to take part in the school fête on the Saturday when you would normally have contact, for example, try to rearrange your visit for another day; suppose that the mother wants to take the children for a fortnight's holiday – she might find it very helpful to rearrange contact so that the holiday could be for an unbroken period; or if the father has to stay away on business when he would normally have had contact, he will want to see the children at another time if possible. If contact arrangements are to remain adaptable, both parents will have to be very co-operative.

3. Even if you have a flexible arrangement for contact, try to fix the details of visits a reasonable time in advance and stick to them exactly. This may not always be possible (for example, one of you may be ill) but if you have to cancel a visit for any reason, try to let the other parent know as soon as possible. Nothing is more upsetting for children than to be in a state of perpetual uncertainty over contact and it is particularly soul destroying for them to be all ready for a day out with their father or mother, who simply fails to turn up without giving any reason, or who cancels arrangements at the last minute.

4. When you only see your child for contact, it is very tempting to spoil him and to let him get away with 'murder'. A little bit of indulgence will probably do no harm at all but you do need to be careful that you do not undermine the other parent's authority in any way or make it difficult for the child to settle back into his everyday routine after contact.

5. If your child has friends in your area with whom he would like to play on contact visits, do not feel that he is obliged to spend the whole day with you. You are free to spend the day in whatever way suits both of you best.

6. Coping with the effects of a contact visit may require some patience from the parent with whom the child lives. Even the best managed visits can disrupt the child's home life and you can expect him to be excited before contact and often a little upset, perhaps even badly behaved, after contact until he has settled down into his routine again. Do not be too quick to blame the other parent for this (or the child) – it may be inevitable.

Staying or visiting contact

(a) *Staying contact:* There will be no prospect of a court permitting you to have your child to stay overnight unless you can provide satisfactory accommodation for him. If you hope to have the child to stay for prolonged periods, you (or someone on your behalf) will have to be able to cope with everyday chores such as washing and ironing the child's clothes. Very young children are perhaps less likely to benefit from staying contact than older children, and babies, especially, may not be able to be away from their mothers overnight. If your child genuinely does not want to stay away overnight, the court would be unlikely to order him to do so.

In the early days after a divorce or after a residence order has been made, your child may need some time to settle down to his new life and it can sometimes be a good idea to let him have a period without staying contact in which to find his feet. However there is usually no reason why regular contact visits should not be arranged during this period so that the child can remain in close contact with you.

If staying contact is arranged and is working well, it can often be increased to quite extensive periods, perhaps up to or exceeding half of each school holiday and one weekend in every two or three.

(b) *Visiting contact:* Staying contact may not be a practical proposition for a variety of reasons. If so, you will have to content yourself with seeing the children during the day and returning them to their mother at night. This can pose something of a problem if you live some way away from the child – if you take the child home for the visit, the whole day will be spent travelling, whereas if you stay in the area all day, you risk the child becoming bored because it is a problem to find suitable entertainment. You should be careful to bear these difficulties in mind when you arrange the time and place where you will collect the child for contact and when and where you will return him. Make sure that the 'pick-up point' that you arrange is convenient for both parents (bearing in mind the public transport available if either of you has to rely on this) and has somewhere where you can wait in comfort if the other parent is delayed. Obviously it will cause the least problems if you can pick the child up at his home. You need not come into contact with the other parent if she keeps an eye open for your arrival and sends the child out when you come. Punctuality is vital when collecting and returning the child – if you are late (or even unduly early) you will probably have to contend with an irate parent and a distraught child!

(c) *Supervised contact:* You may find that even short periods of contact cause problems of one sort or another. It may help if you can arrange for a third party, perhaps a relative whom your child knows, to be present on a few occasions. On the other hand, it is not normally very successful to have both parents present during a contact visit, because both you and your child will probably find it impossible to behave naturally.

If the court is worried about contact, it can sometimes arrange for one or two contact visits to be supervised by an independent person, for example a social worker, to make sure that everything is working out all right.

Alternatively, some areas have special family centres where contact visits can take place with the family centre workers on hand to assist with transferring the child from one parent to the other and with any problems that arise. Sometimes the workers can also provide more continuous supervision on a number of occasions if, for some reason, it is feared that the child may come to harm from the other parent if he has contact with him or her alone.

Do we need to make any firm arrangements for contact at all?

If you live within easy reach of the children and they are old enough to make their own arrangements to come and see you, there is no reason why you should not leave it up to them to pop in and see you whenever they want rather than arranging for contact visits at particular times.

Christmas Day and other special occasions

A lot of bad feeling can be caused over Christmas Day and other special occasions during the year. Christmas Day in particular is very special for both parents and children, and neither parent will want to be without the children on that day. If you live sufficiently close, you may be able to arrange for the children to spend part of the day with each of you. If this is not possible, the fairest way is usually for one parent to have the children on Christmas Day one year (and the other to see them on Christmas Eve or Boxing Day) and the other parent to have them for Christmas Day the next year. If any other days are particularly special for your family, for example birthdays, you could try to come to an arrangement to alternate these in a similar way. If you live close enough to each other, there should be no reason why you cannot arrange a meeting between your child and his other parent so that he can have his birthday present from that parent personally on the day.

Asking the court to resolve disputes over contact

If you are unable to reach agreement over contact you can ask the court to settle the matter for you. It is sometimes convenient for the court to make an order defining contact when it decides the issue as to where the children are to live; in other cases, a separate contact hearing has to be arranged.

If a separate hearing is fixed, you will find that the procedure for preparing the case and at the court itself is much the same as for the residence hearing described in the preceding chapter. However, contact problems can sometimes be dealt with by a district judge rather than by a judge. Whoever decides the case will probably require a welfare report to assist him, just as in a residence dispute.

Like a residence order, a contact order is never final. Either parent can ask the court to reconsider the question if the circumstances warrant this. It is important to realise that even if the court does lay down fixed times for contact, you normally can change these by agreement between you without referring the matter to the court. There is generally no reason why you should not arrange for more contact to take place than the court order provides if you both agree. You cannot, however, either of you alter the times and places or the number of contact visits fixed by the court if the other parent does *not* agree.

PART 5:
REACHING AGREEMENT
ABOUT THE FUTURE

16
Coming to an Agreement over Arrangements for the Future

There are so many things that must be planned when you separate or get divorced. Who is to live in the family home? Who is to pay the mortgage instalments, look after the children, meet the household bills, deal with the school fees?

Some people prefer to make their own arrangements for the future without involving the court. If you can come to an agreement over things yourselves, so much the better – you will both benefit from an amicable arrangement that cuts out the bickering and unpleasantness which often arises if you have to ask the court to sort out your affairs for you.

You may find it impossible to come to terms in the initial stages of separation and divorce and only manage to agree as the court hearing about your property and finances draws near. This chapter is not about that sort of agreement – if you are in that situation, you should refer to Chapter 20. You may want to come to an amicable agreement but find that you get stuck on certain issues. In that case, the help of a trained mediator, skilled in helping couples find common ground, could be invaluable – if you are in that situation, refer to Chapter 17.

Considerations to bear in mind when making an agreement
1. WHAT SHOULD GO INTO THE AGREEMENT?
You can deal with all sorts of matters – your separation, maintenance for yourself and the children (subject to the Child

Support Act 1991, see Chapter 20), payment of a lump sum of money by one of you to the other, details about the house (who is to live there, own it, pay the outgoings, etc.), who is to look after the children, contact with the children and so on. The exact contents of your agreement are up to the two of you. Generally, the more you can resolve in your agreement, the better. But do not be deterred from making an agreement about some matters, just because you cannot agree over everything.

2. WHY MAKE AN AGREEMENT?

You may wonder whether there is any point in making a formal agreement – perhaps you already have an informal arrangement that you have never really discussed but which seems to work reasonably well in practice, or perhaps you have agreed on things in discussion but never got round to writing anything down.

In fact, there can be practical advantages of making a formal arrangement, particularly when it comes to financial matters:

a) *Financial aspects:* a voluntary arrangement is all very well, but have you considered that your wife may be finding it difficult to budget because she cannot be sure what she will receive by way of maintenance from you at the end of the week or month? Have you experienced difficulties in making yourself pay what you know your wife needs because you are hard up yourself?

With a firm agreement, you know exactly what you have to pay and when, and you can budget for it. Your wife knows that she can rely on that sum at regular intervals.

b) *Other aspects:* you may not feel it is so important to record other arrangements in a formal agreement, particularly if they are of the type that are best kept flexible, for example contact arrangements. However, people do quite often like to make a formal agreement to separate, just to put things on a definite basis for the future. Others like to include everything that has been sorted out in the agreement just to tie up all the loose ends.

3. HOW DOES ONE GO ABOUT MAKING AN AGREEMENT?

Agreements should generally be in writing. Agreements by word of mouth only are not a good idea as they can give rise to disputes between you in the future over exactly what was arranged.

Depending on what you have agreed, it may be possible for the agreement simply to be written out clearly, or it may be necessary for it to be embodied in a formal legal deed, signed and sealed in the presence of witnesses. You can also ask your solicitor to translate the terms of your agreement into a court order known as a 'consent order'.

If you do not have your agreement made into a court order, to make sure that your agreement will be binding and effective, it is important that you consult your solicitor. Take his advice on the terms of the agreement. He will make sure that the arrangement you have arrived at is fair and reasonable for you and that the written document that is drawn up really does represent what you both intended. It is usually preferable for each of you to take advice from a separate solicitor over the agreement so that neither of you feels aggrieved, when looking back on the agreement, because the solicitor's advice seemed to favour the other spouse.

4. WHAT THE AGREEMENT CANNOT DO

a) Unless it is in the form of a consent order dismissing any further financial claims, the agreement you reach cannot prevent either of you from subsequently applying to the court to have your financial position reviewed. Some people try to rule out the possibility of such an application by, for example, a term in the agreement that states that the wife undertakes that, provided that her husband pays her the maintenance agreed, she will never apply to the court for further maintenance or for any further share in the family property. Terms such as this are not binding, although if both parties had legal advice at the time they made the agreement, and if all financial details were disclosed, the courts would be inclined to uphold such an agreement.

b) An agreement cannot make arrangements to cope with

the situation *if* you separate at some date in the future. The law looks upon this as an encouragement to you to separate of which it disapproves considering it contrary to public policy. Nevertheless, this does not mean that you have to wait until you have actually separated before you make your agreement – you are quite free to make an agreement *on the occasion of your immediate* separation.

5. CAN THE AGREEMENT EVER BE MADE FINAL?

No arrangements that you make with regard to the children will be final, whatever you agree between the two of you. The court can always step in at the request of either party and change what you have agreed over residence and contact.

If you agree to separate, the court cannot force you to live together again, so in a sense this part of your agreement is final. However, should you decide between you that you would like to give the marriage another try, there is no reason why you should not start to live together again, whatever your agreement says.

If you wish to do so, you *can* make your financial and property arrangements final in so far as they affect the two of you, provided (i) that your arrangements do not involve the payment of maintenance from one of you to the other and (ii) that you are prepared to enlist the help of the court.

Not all couples will want, or be able, to make final arrangements, but for example, a young couple with no children may prefer to make a clean break after their divorce and might arrange that they each take half of all their combined assets and that neither will make any claims on the other for maintenance in the future. Or an older wife, whose children have left home and who is working part-time, might agree to accept all her husband's share in the family home as well as her own, and in return to release him from any obligation to maintain her in the future (as he might have had to do had she taken a smaller share of the family capital).

To make this type of arrangement final, you require a court order (consent order). What happens is that the court makes an order providing for all the matters upon which you have

agreed and then dismisses all the other claims that either of
you might have made on divorce. So, in the case of the young
couple and the older wife, the court would dismiss each wife's
claim to maintenance and would order that the couple's assets
be divided up as they had agreed. The wives would lose their
rights to claim maintenance ever again as soon as the court
order was made.

Considerations whilst the agreement is in force

1. WHAT OBLIGATIONS DO YOU BOTH HAVE?
Whilst the agreement is in force, you are both bound by its
terms. If either of you breaks the agreement, the other can take
steps to have it enforced by the court. You should refer to
Chapter 22 for the procedure whereby agreements can be
enforced.

2. VARYING THE AGREEMENT
a) *If you both agree to the alteration:* there is no reason why
you should not change the terms of your agreement in the
future (for example to increase or decrease the amount of
maintenance payable) if you both agree. Check with your
solicitor whether the variation needs to be put in a formal
deed. If you had the terms of your agreement put into a
consent order and you want the change to be made formal, you
will need to return to court to have it varied (see Chapter 25).

b) *If you do not agree:* the spouse seeking the change may
be able to apply to the court for a new arrangement to be
ordered. As you have seen, the court can always order a
change in relation to arrangements for the children if it feels it
is necessary to do so. As for financial arrangements for the
two of you, unless you have made your arrangement final by a
court order as described in paragraph 5 above, there may be
two ways in which you could have it altered:

(i) if your agreement is in writing and you can show that
circumstances have changed since you made it so that it no
longer makes fair financial provision for you, you can ask the
court to step in and repair the deficiency in the agreement. For

example, it might raise the amount of maintenance you are receiving under the agreement because your husband's salary has gone up substantially. It can even make provisions about finance where the original agreement only dealt with separation and did not mention money at all;

or (ii) if you are going through a divorce and you have not yet had your financial and property position dealt with by the court as part of the divorce proceedings, you can make an application for financial provision and property adjustment orders in the normal way (see Chapter 20) despite your agreement. However, when the court considers your application it will bear in mind the provisions of your agreement, and it will be an uphill (if not impossible) task to persuade the court to make orders that conflict with the terms of your agreement if circumstances have remained unchanged since you made it and you had independent legal advice at the time.

3. HOW LONG WILL THE AGREEMENT LAST?
There are a number of ways in which an agreement can come to an end:

a) *By agreement:* your agreement will terminate in accordance with any time limit that you fixed when you made it. For example, if you agreed that it would continue until your youngest living child reached 18, it will terminate on this event. Alternatively, you can agree after the agreement has been running for a while that it should come to an end. If you do so, it will terminate in accordance with this fresh agreement.

b) *By breach:* if one of you is guilty of a serious failure to observe the terms of the agreement, the other may be free to look upon the agreement as at an end, if he or she wishes to do so. Alternatively, he or she could apply to the court to enforce the agreement (see Chapter 22). It will not be enough that your spouse has simply failed to pay the maintenance he or she agreed to under the agreement on one or two occasions. But if the failure were to continue for a substantial period of time, this might release you from your obligations under the agreement. Your solicitor will advise you when this point is reached.

c) *By beginning to live together again:* if you start to live together again after you have made the agreement, this may or may not put an end to the agreement for good. It will depend on the way in which your agreement is drafted and what you intended to happen in such a situation. You should take your solicitor's advice as to whether it is necessary to make a new agreement if you subsequently separate again.

d) *By death or remarriage:* it may well be provided or implied in the agreement that no financial obligations will exist between you after the death of one of you. So, for example, an agreement for a husband to pay a wife weekly maintenance may cease when he dies so that his estate will have no liability to maintain the wife. It may also be provided or implied that the payment of maintenance should cease if the payee remarries.

17

Would Mediation Assist Me?

Until the relevant part of The Family Law Act 1996 came into force, if parties could not reach agreement about their arrangements upon separation or divorce in the manner described in Chapter 16, the alternative was to go to court. The new legislation provided another option: mediation.

Mediation involves the parties to a marriage attempting to reach their own informed and agreed decisions about arrangements for the future, including any issues between them about children, property or financial matters. A neutral person, the mediator, is there to help. If you participate in mediation you will have a series of meetings with a recognised mediator to discuss arrangements for the future. The mediator will not decide things for you but will help you and your spouse reach your own decisions.

Mediation is an alternative to decision making by the courts. It is not part of the decision making procedures of the courts. Nor does mediation replace legal advice: it is still advisable to have a solicitor who can make sure that the arrangements you have arrived at are fair and reasonable for you and that any written document that is drawn up at the end of the mediation process (be it a formal deed or a consent order) accurately represents what you intended.

When can mediation take place?
Mediation can take place at any time, even before divorce proceedings have begun. It can also be helpful when the divorce took place some time ago but there are still problems, for example over the children.

Types of mediation
Mediators can be either 'family mediators' or 'lawyer mediators' and you will have to decide whether to use one or other type, or both. Family mediators usually have expertise in

social work or mental health and may previously have been counsellors or social workers. They can be particularly helpful if your dispute with your spouse is about the children.

Lawyer mediators are lawyers with expertise in how the courts deal with family matters. They often charge higher fees than family mediators. They can give clients legal information to help them make well informed choices during mediation, and because of their legal background they should be able to ensure that any agreements you can come to about financial matters will hold water. They cannot advise either party *individually*, however, and each of you should still get independent legal advice.

Some mediation services (such as the Family Mediators' Association (FMA) whose details you will find in Chapter 26) offer co-mediation, where a family mediator and a lawyer mediator work together.

What happens if we decide to use mediation?

Both you and your spouse need to attend mediation for it to be effective. You can expect to have about half a dozen sessions, although some people require more, some fewer.

At your first session the mediator will explain what mediation is all about and help you set an agenda covering the issues you and your spouse want to discuss. You may, for example, be in agreement about arrangements for the children but need to resolve financial issues, or you may need 'all-issues' mediation.

If money matters form part of the agenda, both spouses must agree to give full disclosure of their financial situation. You will be required to fill in a form giving details of income, savings, debts, pensions, etc. You will need to send these to the mediator who will then send a copy to the other spouse.

At the next session the mediator will identify whether more information is needed and where there are disagreements between you. Each of you will have the opportunity to put forward possible solutions, and if necessary the mediator will help by suggesting an alternative option.

If an agreement is reached, the mediator will prepare a

'Memorandum of Understanding' summarising the agreement for each spouse and his or her solicitor. Your solicitors can double-check the terms of the agreement before it is written up into a formal deed or consent order.

Will my case be suitable for mediation?

There are many advantages to sorting our your affairs without fighting it out in court, whether you use the mediation process or simply come to an agreement. For one thing, you are much more likely to resolve your problems in an amicable way. This is particularly beneficial to any children involved. Also, you will have been much more in control of your future arrangements; had you gone to court, a judge would have imposed arrangements on you. Furthermore, if you successfully resolve matters in this way it could save you considerable time and money.

However, there are some cases which are unsuitable for mediation for a variety of reasons, for example, where:

(i) either you or your spouse is unwilling to negotiate;

(ii) there is extreme conflict between you, or one of you cannot stand up for yourself against the other;

(iii) either of you suffers from a major mental or physical disability;

(iv) criminal or child protection issues are involved;

(v) one of you has no confidence in the other one's ability to keep to any agreement.

If the mediator considers your case unsuitable for mediation, and agreement cannot be reached, your solicitor will have to act for you in the traditional way and where appropriate help you to apply for public funding for court proceedings.

What if mediation breaks down?

Mediation might help you successfully resolve all your issues, you might only partially sort out your arrangements for the future, or mediation might break down altogether. If there are issues outstanding, your solicitor will help you to apply for public funding (if you are financially eligible) to provide you with legal representation for court proceedings.

Is public funding available to pay for mediation?

Yes, for those who are financially eligible. Indeed, to encourage people to use this service instead of going to court, you will not have to make a financial contribution, and you cannot be required to pay back public funding under a Help with Mediation certificate, whereas you can be required to pay back other types of public funding by virtue of the 'statutory charge' (see Chapter 4).

How to find a mediation service

To find out about mediation services in your area, you can contact the Family Mediators' Association (see Chapter 26 for details). Alternatively, your solicitor or local Citizens' Advice Bureau should be able to give you the address of your nearest mediation service.

PART 6:
FINANCIAL ARRANGEMENTS

18
Preventing your Spouse from Running off with all the Family Assets

Normally, when a divorce takes place, the couple concerned decide between them what should happen to their house and other property after the divorce or, if they cannot agree, they refer the matter to the court for a decision as to who is to have what.

Sometimes, however, one spouse is not prepared to play by the rules, and when he realises that a divorce is inevitable, makes plans to dispose of all the family finance and property so that the other spouse cannot lay any claim to it. For example, a husband may decide to sell the house without his wife's consent and fritter away the proceeds or transfer them out of the country. Or he may give away all his valuable assets to his mistress to prevent his wife from getting her hands on them.

This chapter outlines the steps that can be taken to prevent a spouse from successfully escaping from his or her financial obligations after the divorce in this way. Whilst the chapter assumes that it is the husband who is attempting to shirk his responsibilities, the same principles apply if the wife attempts to defeat her husband's claims by making dispositions of her property.

1. The home: precautionary measures
In many cases, the family house will be not only your major asset but also the only place you have to live. It will therefore

be vital to make sure that your husband cannot sell it without your consent.

If your name is on the title deeds of the property, there is no risk of your spouse disposing of it in any way without your knowledge. He will need your consent and your signature before he can mortgage the property or transfer it to anyone else by sale or gift.

Whilst it is likely that you would find out if your husband was trying to sell the house in which you are living, nevertheless, if the house is in your husband's sole name, he could theoretically conclude a deal without telling you anything about it because he will not need your consent or your signature to do so. To protect you against the risk of your husband dealing with the house in any way, against your will, your solicitor will probably consider registering a 'notice' or 'land charge'. Whenever a house is sold, a prospective purchaser makes various enquiries before he decides definitely that he will buy. As part of these enquiries, he will consult a register which shows whether anyone else has any rights in respect of the property. Your land charge or notice shows on this register that you have the right to occupy the property because you are married to the owner of it. A purchaser would be very unlikely to go ahead and buy the property once he found out about this and, even if he did, he may have to allow you to go on living there for some time.

2. Seeking protection from the court: the home and other assets

If you can satisfy the court:

(i) that you have a claim to a share of the family assets or income

and (ii) that your spouse is about to make off with some of the assets to defeat your claim, or has already done so, the court may be able to step in and prevent the proposed dispositions taking place or set aside whatever transactions your spouse has already completed.

If you are seriously worried that your spouse is contemplating some sort of deal which will work to your disadvantage, contact your solicitor *without delay*. There is far more that he can do to help you before the deal actually takes place than after it has been accomplished.

a) *Before the deal takes place*

The court can make an injunction to prevent your spouse from disposing of any of his or the family's assets, for example savings in the bank account, a valuable piece of furniture or the house itself. Disobedience to an injunction is punishable ultimately by imprisonment.

Alternatively the court can make an order that your spouse pay over money that he has to an independent person for safe keeping, for example into an account at the court or a bank account in the names of both your solicitors.

b) *After the deal has taken place*

You may not find out about your husband's activities until after he has put a large proportion of his assets out of your reach. Whether the court can then do anything to help you will depend on the circumstances in which your husband has disposed of the assets. The court has the power to set transactions aside, but only provided that they were not made with someone who paid a proper price and had no idea of your claim and your husband's intention to defeat it. Obviously it would be unfair if an honest person such as this, who had paid · for the particular item, were to be deprived of it at a later stage.

To give you an example, suppose that your husband puts all his stocks and shares into the name of his mother who pays him nothing for them and knows exactly what is going on – the court could set this transaction aside. Suppose however that your husband sells the stocks and shares to ordinary purchasers (who have no idea of the circumstances) and dissipates the proceeds – there is nothing the court can do to recover the stocks and shares for you.

19
Obtaining Financial Help Before Your Divorce Comes Through

As your marriage breaks down, you could find yourself facing pressing financial problems. If you have earnings or savings of your own, you may be able to cope, at least until a permanent financial agreement can be reached after the divorce. But some problems just will not wait. It is usually the wife who does not have independent resources and who suffers most acutely in the early stages if, for example, her husband stops paying her any housekeeping money or refuses to meet the household bills or to pay the mortgage. This chapter therefore assumes that it is the wife who will be seeking financial help; a husband would however be eligible to make an application to the court for maintenance from his wife or to claim state benefits in exactly the same way if he needed to do so.

Coping with your immediate problems
To begin with you will probably have to rely on whatever savings you have managed to accumulate and on borrowing whatever you can from relatives and friends. Whilst this may enable you to meet day to day living expenses, major bills such as the mortgage payments, gas and electricity are likely to remain a problem. Do not be afraid to approach the building society or authority concerned and explain your situation to them quite frankly – you will be surprised how sympathetic and accommodating they are in most cases.

Sooner or later, however, you will need assistance of a more positive kind. You may be able to agree a maintenance arrangement with your husband for the short term, but if he is unreliable there is no way of enforcing the payments. If you are not able to make a voluntary arrangement which reliably meets your financial needs, there are two other ways in which you may be able to obtain help at this stage – by applying to the court for an order obliging your husband to maintain you and by applying for benefits of a social security nature such as income support.

State and other benefits

There are various kinds of cash help available. You can obtain information about the benefits currently available from your local social security office or jobcentre and from the Department for Work and Pensions (DWP) helpline and website (for details see Chapter 26).

The chart on page 131 shows the benefits that are most likely to help you. None of them depends on whether you have made national insurance contributions. The chart assumes that you and your husband are living separately, even though you are not yet divorced.

If you are in financial difficulty whilst still living with your spouse, you should seek advice about state benefits from a Citizens' Advice Bureau or from your local Social Security office. You may, for example, be able to arrange for your husband's income support to be paid to you instead of to him, if he is refusing to support you and the children properly. You yourself should also be able to draw any child benefit to which your family is entitled unless you have specifically assigned your right to do so to your husband.

Court orders

The help you can obtain through the courts depends on whether you or your spouse have yet started divorce proceedings. This chapter deals with the orders that can be made in your own favour. You will find information about maintenance for children in Chapter 20, Part III.

1. If you or your spouse have already started divorce proceedings

WHAT TYPE OF HELP CAN I GET?

The divorce court can order your husband to make regular cash payments to you to provide for your needs until the divorce comes through. Such payments are commonly referred to as 'maintenance'. Because the court's order is only temporary as yet, the official term for the maintenance ordered is 'maintenance pending suit' (in other words, maintenance before decree absolute is granted). Because it will add to the overall cost of the case, unless the maintenance is going to be significantly higher than state benefit, an application for maintenance pending suit may not be cost effective. However, the fact that the court has power to make such an order sometimes produces an offer to pay on an interim basis.

The court cannot order your husband to pay you a more substantial lump sum of money or deal with the ownership of your property (the house, furniture, car, etc.) at this point; that will be sorted out after your divorce comes through. The court may, however, be able to make orders as to who is to live in the house if it is not possible for both of you to go on living there together (see Chapter 12). The court can also take steps to prevent either of you from disposing of any of your property before it has had the opportunity to consider what should be done with it in the future, if it feels that what you propose to do with the property will restrict its powers to achieve a fair long term arrangement for you both (see Chapter 18).

DOES IT MATTER WHO STARTED THE DIVORCE PROCEEDINGS?
It does not matter whether you or your husband started the divorce proceedings – either of you can apply for maintenance pending suit. It is no advantage to you when you apply for maintenance to be the one who started the divorce proceedings; your maintenance will not be increased if you are claiming a divorce or decreased if you are being divorced. Nor is the way you have both behaved relevant to the issues of finance or property unless one of you has behaved so badly that most right thinking people would consider it unfair that that spouse should receive a normal amount of maintenance or should still get his or her normal share in the family property.

Type of benefit	Do I qualify?	What form does the benefit take?	Further information and how to apply
1. Income support	If you are a lone parent looking after children under 16 and are working fewer than 16 hours per week, you may qualify. The government's 'New Deal for Lone Parents' provides extra allowances and incentives to help to get you into work. Capital can affect your entitlement.	Generally you receive a regular cash payment. There is a premium for one-parent families. You may be entitled to help with rent (see paragraph 5 below) or the interest element of mortgage payments (limited to a £100,000 loan after 8-39 weeks have elapsed). You will automatically be entitled to help with health costs (dental treatment, prescriptions) and Legal Help (see Chapter 4).	Contact your local social security office or visit the Department for Work and Pensions (DWP) website (see Chapter 26). You will be asked to attend a 'work-focused interview' with a personal adviser, but will not necessarily have to seek work. The *New Deal for Lone Parents* provides extra allowances for lone parents, with incentives and help intended to get you into work.
2. Jobseeker's allowance	If you are unemployed or work fewer than 16 hours per week you may be eligible.	You will receive a regular cash payment, and you will be eligible for many of the same benefits as claimants of income support.	Contact your social security office or visit the DWP website (see above). You will have to attend an interview and draw up a Jobseeker's Agreement with the interviewer.

Type of benefit	Do I qualify?	What form does the benefit take?	Further information and how to apply
3. Working tax credit	If you are working at least 16 hours per week and look after at least one child, you may be eligible if your earnings and capital fall below a certain level.	You can receive a regular cash payment or a tax credit made through your wage packet. The credit will be assessed and paid on a six monthly basis. You will also be entitled to help with health costs, etc. (see income support).	Contact your local Inland Revenue or social security office, or ring the Tax Credits Helpline on 0845 300 3900.
4. Child tax credit	If you are responsible for at least one child, whether you are working or not, you may be eligible if your income and capital fall below a certain level.	You can receive a regular cash payment or a tax credit made through your wage packet. The credit will be assessed and paid on a six monthly basis. You will also be entitled to help with health costs, etc.	Contact your local Inland Revenue or social security office, or ring the Tax Credits Helpline (as above).
5. Housing benefit and council tax benefit	If you have difficulty in paying your rent or council tax, whether or not you are in work, you may be eligible for assistance. Whether you do receive help with your rent or council tax will depend on your personal circumstances – your income, capital, whether you are on income support/jobseeker's allowance, the amount of rent you pay, how many children you have living with you, etc. Both council and private tenants are eligible for help with rent and even owner occupiers can get help with council tax.	If you are a private tenant, you receive a rent allowance in cash. Council tenants receive help in the form of a reduction in the rent they have to pay. Council tax benefit takes the form of a reduction in the amount of council tax you pay.	Contact your local social security office or local council. If you claim income support or jobseeker's allowance, claim forms for housing benefit and council tax will be included.

Type of benefit	Do I qualify?	What form does the benefit take?	Further information and how to apply
6. Child benefit	If you are responsible for a child under 16, or under 19 and still studying at school, you should be eligible for child benefit. You can claim if the child is living with you or if you contribute towards his maintenance at a rate of at least the current child benefit rate. This could mean that either you or your husband could be eligible for the benefit. In these circumstances it is usual for the parent with whom the child is living to draw the benefit.	You can draw a regular fixed sum for each relevant child. If you were on benefits and already looking after a child on your own in July 1998 and you have now come off benefits and started working, ask your social security office whether you are entitled to an uplift in child benefit known as *lone parent benefit*.	Contact your local social security or Inland Revenue office or visit the DWP website (see Chapter 26).

WHEN DO I APPLY?
You can apply at any stage between the commencement of the
divorce proceedings (when the divorce petition is filed with
the court – see Chapter 8) and the date on which decree nisi of
divorce is made absolute, whether or not you are living apart.

HOW LONG DOES AN ORDER FOR MAINTENANCE PENDING SUIT
LAST?
Maintenance pending suit is only designed as a temporary
measure to tide you over until your divorce is finalised and
long term plans for your property and finances can be made
and put into operation. Maintenance pending suit therefore
ceases to be payable when your divorce is made absolute
though it can be replaced by interim periodical payments if
you have still not obtained a final order dealing with your
finances by that stage.

HOW MUCH MAINTENANCE WILL I GET?
It is not possible to tell you exactly how much maintenance
pending suit you will get. A maintenance order is tailor made
for you – it all depends on your personal income and requirements. Your application is considered by a district judge who
has to decide what maintenance would be reasonable in your
case.

WHAT SORT OF CONSIDERATIONS ARE RELEVANT TO THE DIS-
TRICT JUDGE'S DECISION?
The district judge will look at the circumstances of both of
you and concentrate on achieving a fair balance between
what you need to provide a roof over your head and to look
after your everyday needs and what your husband can afford
to pay. You will both be expected to provide details of your
income from all sources (earnings, child benefit, interest
from savings accounts, etc.) and your regular expenses (food,
heating, rent, mortgage, school dinners for the children, etc.).
Assessing your income and expenses is not always completely straightforward. The following points quite often
arise:

a) You may already be receiving social security benefits of a kind that depend on your means, for example income support. These will not be counted as part of your steady income because as soon as you start to receive maintenance, your means go up and your social security benefits may therefore be reduced. Nevertheless, the district judge can rely on the fact that, if your husband cannot afford to pay you anything at all, perhaps because he is unemployed, you will be provided for by the State.

b) You may have formed a relationship with another man. If you *live* with him, he will probably help to provide for your everyday needs, for example you may live in his house instead of having to pay your own rent, electricity bills, etc., or he may pay for food for the family or for your petrol or clothes. If you have this kind of relationship your need for maintenance from your husband will be reduced and you will find that you may no longer be eligible for maintenance or that the order you get will be very much reduced.

c) Resources available to you or your husband will not always take the form of money. Other resources can be taken into account such as board and lodging provided free with your job, luncheon vouchers, a company car.

If you want to get a rough idea of whether you would be entitled to any maintenance pending suit, you can draw up a balance sheet setting out your monthly or weekly income and your reasonable outgoings for the same period. If your income already equals or exceeds your expenses, you are unlikely to get maintenance pending suit although it is still worth asking your solicitor about it. If your income is less than your outgoings, you may well be eligible for maintenance pending suit provided that your husband is in a position to make payments to you (he may not be if, for example, he is unemployed). Your solicitor will have a look at all the figures and tell you whether you are likely to get an order. Because there is no mathematical formula for working out maintenance pending suit, he will not necessarily be able to tell you exactly what will be ordered, but he will be able to give you a good idea from his experience of cases such as yours.

You will find that some of the information provided in the following chapter on long term maintenance (periodical payments) is also relevant to your application for maintenance pending suit. However, you should bear in mind that whereas an order for periodical payments is made after a detailed consideration of all your circumstances and is usually meant to last for some considerable time, an order for maintenance pending suit is temporary and the district judge may have to do the best he can to be fair on the limited information that is available so far about your circumstances. This may not include all the details he would like to know when he considers periodical payments. You can therefore often expect a maintenance pending suit order to be for rather less than a periodical payments order would be.

INTERIM MAINTENANCE PENDING SUIT

It sometimes happens that the district judge is not in a position to make a maintenance pending suit order when he first considers your application. This can be for a variety of reasons, for example, he may not yet have sufficient information about your husband's financial position or he may feel that your case involves a complication that should be referred to a judge to decide. Should this be the case, the district judge can, if you need immediate help, make an even more temporary order called an 'interim maintenance pending suit order'. This is based on whatever evidence is available so far and lasts only until the court can consider your application for maintenance pending suit fully. You cannot expect an interim order to be more than rough and ready assistance to get you out of difficulties for the immediate future.

2. If neither of you has yet commenced divorce proceedings

If neither of you has yet started divorce proceedings, you will not be able to apply to the divorce court for maintenance pending suit. Nevertheless, there are other ways in which you can obtain assistance from the courts; the magistrates' court can be particularly helpful in these circumstances.

WHAT ORDERS CAN THE MAGISTRATES' COURT (FAMILY PROCEEDINGS PANEL) MAKE ABOUT FINANCE?

In order to obtain help with your financial situation from a magistrates' court, you must be able to show that you are eligible for a magistrates' court order. The chart below sets out the ways in which you can qualify for an order and the type of order that can be made.

If you can prove that:	*You can obtain an order for:*
i) your husband has deserted you	maintenance for yourself (payable weekly or at any other interval) and/or a lump sum payment of not more than £1,000 and/or a lump sum payment of not more than £1,000 for a child.
ii) your husband has behaved unreasonably	
iii) your husband has failed to provide reasonable maintenance for you	
iv) your husband has failed to provide or make reasonable contribution towards the maintenance of a child of the family	
v) you and your husband have come to a financial arrangement that you would both like the court to put into an order	maintenance for yourself in the form you have agreed and/or a lump sum payment of the amount you have agreed upon (which can exceed £1,000).

HOW DO THE MAGISTRATES DECIDE ON THE AMOUNT OF THE ORDER?

The magistrates will fix the amount of maintenance they order in much the same way as the divorce court decides on the amount of periodical payments you should receive after your divorce (see Chapter 20). The amount of any lump sum will depend on what you need, what expenses you incurred in maintaining yourself before you made your application to the court, and how much your husband can afford to pay.

WHAT IF WE ARE STILL LIVING TOGETHER?

If you are living together when you make your application to the magistrates' court, you can still obtain an order from the court. However, if you go on living together for a continuous period of more than six months after the order is made, an order for maintenance will cease to be effective.

If you are living apart when you get an order but you subsequently start to live together again, your maintenance order will cease if you live together for a continuous period of more than six months.

If you require maintenance at any stage after your maintenance order has ceased, you will have to apply to the court again.

CAN THE COUNTY COURT MAKE AN ORDER BEFORE DIVORCE PROCEEDINGS HAVE BEGUN?

In theory the county court can make an order under s27 of the Matrimonial Causes Act before divorce proceedings have begun. However, it costs less to apply to the magistrates' court. If you were applying for public funding for this type of application, the Legal Services Commission would ask your solicitor to justify why the county court would be preferable to the magistrates'.

3. The relationship between maintenance pending suit and magistrates' orders

WHAT IF WE ARE THINKING OF GETTING DIVORCED – IS IT WORTH APPLYING FOR A MAGISTRATES' COURT ORDER?

It really depends on your particular circumstances. If you are about to start divorce proceedings, you will probably be wasting your time applying to the magistrates' court – it would be better to get on with starting the divorce proceedings and apply for maintenance pending suit from the divorce court. If you really are not sure what to do about a divorce and some time is likely to elapse before you are ready to start divorce proceedings, you may need to apply to the magistrates' court meanwhile. Your solicitor will advise you as to the best course to take.

DO I NEED TO INVOLVE THE DIVORCE COURT IN MY FINANCES IF I ALREADY HAVE A MAGISTRATES' COURT ORDER FOR MAINTENANCE WHEN I OR MY HUSBAND START DIVORCE PROCEEDINGS?

Whether you need to do anything further to tide you over until after the divorce will depend on your circumstances. If you are satisfied with the magistrates' order, you can rely on that until the divorce court sorts out your property and finance after the divorce. If you require more than you are getting under the magistrates' court order, your solicitor will advise you as to whether you should return to the magistrates' court to have your order put up or apply to the divorce court for maintenance pending suit.

Once your divorce comes through you will normally want the divorce court to sort out your long term arrangements over property and finance for you. Therefore, whilst your magistrates' court order will not automatically end when you are divorced, it is usually convenient for the divorce court to terminate the magistrates' court order and itself reconsider at that stage the whole question of your finances and property.

If the magistrates' court order should continue after your divorce, maintenance will nevertheless cease to be payable if you, the recipient, then remarry.

An order for a lump sum payment made by the magistrates is normally a 'once and for all' order and is not affected by anything that occurs after it has been paid, be it living together, a divorce or your remarrying.

20

Long Term Arrangements over Property and Finance

What to do about the house, how to share out your other property and how to make sure that you both have sufficient income for the future will no doubt be questions that have been preying on your mind since you first realised that your marriage was at an end.

If you and your spouse are able to come to an agreement about some or all of these questions, so much the better. You should find Chapter 16 helpful in pointing out some of the practical matters that you need to consider in relation to your agreement. As you will see, it is prudent to have your agreement made formal by means of a court order so that there can be no disagreement in the future about its terms and so that you can be sure that you are both bound by it.

If you cannot immediately agree as to what should happen, you could consider whether mediation might assist you to avoid litigation. You will find helpful information about the mediation process in Chapter 17.

If mediation is not suitable for you, or you still cannot agree about your financial matters, you will need to apply for financial orders. You will find an outline of the court procedures – which include a further opportunity to resolve your affairs by agreement at the Financial Dispute Resolution appointment – at Part IV of this chapter.

The majority of cases are resolved at some point without resort to a final hearing, but if you are not able to settle your case by agreement you can ask the court to decide for you. It is normally the job of a district judge of the divorce court to consider your case and formulate your future arrangements for you. His final order (which is often called an 'ancillary relief order') will be tailor-made for you. There is no universal formula that you can use to work out what will be decided in

your case. However, this chapter will give you a guide as to
the sort of solution the court might impose for your problems.
If you feel that you would like more personal advice, your
solicitor should be able to make an assessment of the likely
outcome of the case for you. However, even he can never be
certain what the court will decide because the scope of
potential court orders is so wide.

How to use this chapter
This chapter is divided into four parts.

Part I outlines the wide range of orders that the district
judge can make when he or she considers your case.

Part II describes the considerations that the district judge
will take into account and indicates how he or she might
approach particular problems that arise.

Part III concerns child support maintenance.

Part IV deals with the procedures you need to follow to get
a court order.

PART I. THE ORDERS THAT THE COURT CAN MAKE

The court has far-reaching powers to adjust your rights to
property and income after the divorce to make sure that proper
provision is made for the whole family. The range of potential
orders comprises two categories:

(1) orders concerned with income and with the payment of
lump sums of money (often referred to as 'financial provision
orders');

(2) orders concerned with the family's capital assets (often
referred to as 'property adjustment orders').

(1) Financial provision orders
FOR HUSBAND AND WIFE: there are three types of financial
provision order that the court can make:

(a) an order for periodical payments. This is commonly
known as a 'maintenance order'. It obliges one spouse to pay
the other a sum of money at regular intervals, usually every
week or every month. The payment is normally designed to go

towards living expenses. An order for periodical payments will end automatically on the death or remarriage of the recipient or on the death of the payer.

(b) an order for secured periodical payments. This is an order for maintenance coupled with an order that the payer of the maintenance should guarantee the payments in some way, for example by setting aside assets, such as shares, that will produce sufficient income to cover the maintenance ordered. It will end automatically if the recipient dies or remarries, but it will not necessarily end on the death of the payer. The courts do not often make orders for secured periodical payments unless the family concerned is fairly wealthy.

(c) a lump sum order. This is an order whereby one spouse is ordered to pay the other a lump sum. It is different from the payment of maintenance because it is generally a 'once-and-for-all' payment (although it can sometimes be handed over in instalments), whereas maintenance imposes a continuing obligation to pay at regular intervals over a period of time.

At one time the court could only make a lump sum order as part of a final order. However, the Family Law Act 1996 enabled the courts to make a lump sum order at a later date if it brings to an end a maintenance order. So, for example, if a husband has been paying maintenance to his ex-wife and now wishes to have a clean break, he can apply to the court for an order which ends his obligation to pay her maintenance by compensating her with a large lump sum instead (which she can, if she wishes, invest to create an income).

(d) an earmarking or pension sharing order. These orders divide up pension rights between the parties on divorce. An earmarking order obliges the pension trustees to allocate part of the pension to be paid at retirement to the other spouse. If divorce proceedings began in or after December 2000, the court can make a pension sharing order, whereby part of the value of one spouse's pension can be transferred on divorce to the other, to fund their own pension. It is different from an earmarking order because it can take effect at the time of the final order, allowing a clean break between the parties, whereas an earmarking order does not take effect until the spouse with the pension retires.

FOR THE CHILDREN: since the Child Support Act 1991 came into force the court has no longer had the power to fix the level of maintenance for children. However, if the parents can agree a level of child support maintenance, the terms of their agreement can be put into a 'consent order' (which can later be varied by the court). If the parents cannot agree, the parent with care of the children can apply to the Child Support Agency for an assessment of maintenance. See Part III of this chapter for more details.

The courts retain the power to make lump sum orders in favour of children. This power can normally only be used in relation to children who are under 18 but older children can benefit where either they are still being educated or trained or there are special circumstances. In practice, lump sum orders are seldom made for children unless the child's family is relatively wealthy or the child has a special need for capital.

(2) Property adjustment orders

FOR HUSBAND AND WIFE: the court's powers are so far-reaching in relation to property that, basically, it can reallocate all your property (house, furniture, shares etc., etc.) between you in whatever way it sees fit. For example, it can order one of you to transfer property that you own to the other or to share it with your spouse or to settle it on trust for your spouse or to sell it and divide the proceeds between you and so on.

FOR THE CHILDREN: the court can even allocate some of your property to your children if this seems appropriate. However, most families cannot afford to benefit the children directly in this way as they need all their assets to provide for themselves and the children (for a home, furnishings, etc.) after the divorce. The court will therefore only contemplate transferring some of your assets to your children if you are very well off.

PART II. THE COURT'S APPROACH TO THE PROBLEM

1. Taking stock

The court will need to know exactly what assets and earning power you have between you and what you are both going to need for the future by way of capital and income.

Before the process of sorting out your financial affairs begins, you may find it helpful to draw up a balance sheet listing your joint assets and requirements in two columns: 'Assets' and 'Needs'. In your assets column, you will have to list two kinds of asset – *capital* assets such as your house (whether you own or rent it), car, furniture, savings, insurance policies, business interests, pensions, etc., and *income* which will probably be mainly from your employment but may also be derived from investments, etc.

You will need to put a value on your capital assets. A rough guide may be sufficient with assets such as the contents of the house but the court will require a more exact estimate with more valuable items such as the house itself. Your solicitor will normally be able to arrange for a formal valuation of the house by an estate agent if necessary (or you can) and he may well be able to agree with your spouse or his or her solicitor that you will both abide by the valuation of one estate agent and share his charges rather than going to the expense of obtaining two separate valuations. You will need to know how much is outstanding on your mortgage that you took in order to purchase the house – details of this can be obtained from your bank or building society. You will also have to bear in mind that, if you intend to sell the house, you will have to meet legal and estate agent's fees in respect of the sale.

Consider whether each of your assets could be easily realised if necessary – some may not be realisable, for example, you may have the use of a company car but obviously would not be able to transfer the car to your spouse or sell it even if you wanted to, or you may have business assets that you could not sell without damaging your business. If you have any loans or credit card or other debts, you will need to know the amounts outstanding on those.

In your needs column, it is likely that the major requirements of both of you will be a home (together with furnishings
and furniture) and sufficient income after tax on which to live.

2. Finding a starting point for the court's order

If you asked the court to determine a dispute between you and
your neighbour as to, say, who was entitled to use a particular
strip of land on your joint boundary, the court would decide
the question simply by examining the evidence to see which of
you actually owned the land. Considerations of whether it was
fair that the person owned the land and who *needed* it most
would not enter into the decision.

When you ask the court to determine what should happen to
your family assets and income after your divorce however, the
court has a free hand to do whatever is fair and practical.
Instead of being the *only* consideration, the question of ownership becomes merely one of the many factors that the court
can take into account in reaching its decision, and not a very
important factor at that. This means that, for example, even if
the family home is in the husband's name alone, the wife will
normally be entitled to a share in its value on divorce – indeed,
if necessary, the court can order that it should be transferred
into her name entirely. The same is true of all the family's
assets.

With such a wide scope, how does the district judge know
where to start? There is nothing precise or scientific about the
decision at all – it all depends on the particular circumstances
of the individual family, and it is not possible to say here how
a particular case would be dealt with. However, the law does
direct the district judge's attention to certain matters which are
dealt with in the following sections of this part of the chapter.

Where there are children, the district judge's first priority
will be to ensure that they are properly looked after. Even
where child support maintenance has not actually been calcu-
lated by the Child Support Agency, the level at which it would
assess it will give everyone concerned a starting point for
examining how much is left for dividing between the husband
and wife. Where the children are going to live and with whom

is a very important factor in deciding what should be done with the family home.

You may have heard people talk about something called 'the clean break'. At one time in a typical family, income was provided by the husband and the wife stayed at home looking after him and the children for a substantial part of the marriage. Then, it was contemplated that she would continue to be dependent on the husband for maintenance if they divorced. These days many more wives continue to work throughout much of their marriage and contribute a significant proportion of the family income. Courts, and divorcing couples, now generally prefer a 'clean break' after divorce if possible, with neither spouse dependent on the other for maintenance. As a result, long-term maintenance is less often ordered now, although it is more commonly ordered to last for a fixed period of time during which the wife can retrain with a view to getting back to work if she has been out of the job market for a while.

There are other cases where a clean break between spouses is not appropriate. For example, after a long-standing marriage, a middle aged wife who has never worked outside the home will not be expected to do so after divorce, and the court may well order long term maintenance.

3. The considerations that the court has to bear in mind
The law provides that in deciding on the orders it should make, the court should give first consideration to the welfare during their childhood of any children of the family who are under 18 but must also take into account all the circumstances of the case. In the case of provision for a husband or wife, these circumstances include:

a) the income, earning capacity, property and other financial resources which each of you has or is likely to have in the foreseeable future;

b) the financial needs, obligations and responsibilities that each of you has or is likely to have in the foreseeable future;

c) the standard of living that you enjoyed as a family before the breakdown of your marriage;

d) how old you both are and how long the marriage has lasted;

e) any physical or mental disabilities that either of you has;

f) the contributions that you have both made or are likely to make in the foreseeable future to the welfare of the family (not only financial contributions but also, for example, contributions by looking after the home and caring for the family);

g) whether either of you will lose the chance of acquiring any benefit (for example a widow's pension) as a result of the divorce;

h) in some cases, the conduct of each of you.

Remarriage is not one of the circumstances that the court is specifically directed to take into account. Nevertheless, it can be relevant to the court's decision and you should see Chapter 24 for a summary of the effects of remarriage and the prospect of remarriage on orders of the court in relation to property and finance.

INCOME AND EARNING CAPACITY

(i) *Income.* The court will look at the income of each of you before and after tax, taking into account the expenses that you incur to earn it (for example, National Insurance Contributions, travelling expenses, etc.). If you are employed, your income will be apparent from your past pay slips. If you are self-employed, the court will have a look at your past years' accounts. If you receive state benefits that are not means-tested, these will be taken into account (for example, child benefit). On the other hand, benefits that depend on your means, such as income support, will generally be ignored because they will be affected by whatever order the court makes.

(ii) *Perks.* Some employees receive perks from their employers, for instance the use of a company car, luncheon vouchers, a regular Christmas bonus, etc. Self-employed people often derive similar advantages in kind through their businesses. The court can take this kind of advantage into account.

(iii) *The unemployed husband.* If a man is unemployed through no fault of his own, the court will not make an order that he would only be able to afford to pay from regular earnings. On the other hand, if he is voluntarily out of work and there is employment available to him if he chose to take it, the court might decide to put pressure on him to go back to work by, say, making a maintenance order that he could only afford to pay if he was earning a regular wage.

(iv) *Can a wife be made to work?* It is within the court's power to decide that a wife should receive reduced or no maintenance or to grant her maintenance for a limited period only because she should be working. However, it will never do this unless it is clear that there are jobs available that she could do.

If employment is available for the wife, the court will not penalise her for not taking it until it has gone into all the circumstances. It will look at your past arrangements about work. If, with the husband's agreement, the wife has never worked during the marriage, the court will not necessarily ask her to go out and get a job just because she has got divorced. On the other hand, if she has got a job, she will not be able to give it up and rely on her husband to support her after the divorce. Furthermore, if she is young with no children and can get a job, she will generally be expected to do so – the courts encourage arrangements that can achieve a completely clean break between husband and wife.

If there are children who need looking after, this will obviously affect the wife's ability to work. It is generally accepted that the wife is entitled to stay at home to look after young children unless, of course, she has previously been accustomed to working *and* bringing up the family during the marriage. This may mean that she cannot work at all, or that she can only be expected to do a part time job.

(v) *The resources of a new partner.* If either of you remarries or starts to live with a new partner, this will obviously affect your financial position for better or worse. The court will not give your former spouse a share in the income or assets of your new partner. However, if your new partner pools his or her resources with you, you may find that you have more income and assets available to maintain your former spouse and children. This will be taken into account.

NEEDS AND OBLIGATIONS ETC.:

(i) *A home.* Both of you will probably need a home for yourself (and the children). The court will concentrate very much on making sure that everyone has a roof over their head for the future.

(ii) *Mortgages and loans.* In making arrangements for your future you may well run into debt. If you have had to borrow money for reasonable purposes, for instance to buy yourself somewhere to live, the court will take account of the fact that you will have to repay this sum with interest.

(iii) *Obligations to a new partner.* Far from providing you with additional resources, your new partner may be a drain on your income. You may need to provide him or her with a home, housekeeping, etc. The court will take this into account in assessing your position but will look upon your obligations to your former family as equally important.

(iv) *Ensuring you both have enough income for your needs.* Where a couple has a very low income between them, the court will have to concentrate particularly on providing for their essential needs. The court will make sure that, if it orders one spouse to maintain the other, this will not reduce that spouse's income for his own needs below subsistence level. If this means that he cannot be ordered to pay the other spouse sufficient for her needs, she will have to rely on state benefits to make up the shortfall.

HOW LONG THE MARRIAGE HAS LASTED: Obviously a wife with no children to look after who has been married for only a short time has less right to call on her husband for continuing maintenance and a share in his capital assets than a wife who has been married for some years and has brought up or is bringing up children. A young wife with no children after a short marriage can often only expect to get out of the marriage the equivalent of what she put into it. In other words, she will be entitled to a share in the capital assets only if she contributed to them financially or by her own efforts (for example, by helping with building work involved in improving a house) and will be unlikely to receive maintenance.

YOUR CONTRIBUTIONS TO THE WELFARE OF THE FAMILY: Many couples make equal contributions to family life, although in different ways. Often the wife makes her contribution by caring for the family and the husband makes his by working and contributing financially. In some cases however, one spouse makes a greater contribution than the other, for example because he or she had substantial assets before the marriage or because he or she inherits from a relative during the marriage. In such a situation, it may well be fair for that spouse to take a larger share of the family assets when the marriage breaks down.

THE CONDUCT OF BOTH OF YOU: When a marriage breaks down, a fair share of the blame usually attaches to both parties. So in most cases, the way in which you have both behaved will not affect the court's decision on your property or maintenance. However, there are situations in which conduct can affect the court's order. If one of you has behaved so badly that most ordinary people would feel that he or she should not receive as much income or property as usual, the court can adjust its order appropriately. For example, in one case, the court ordered a husband to transfer all his interest in the house to his wife because he had savaged her with a knife causing her serious injuries. Adultery plain and simple will not normally affect the order. However, it may do so if it occurs in particularly unpleasant circumstances (and possibly if it actually brings about the end of the marriage). So, for example, the court has, in the past, taken into account that a husband had committed adultery with his daughter-in-law.

4. Coping with particular problems

a) THE HOUSE

(i) *If one or both of you own the house (whether or not subject to a mortgage):*
When it comes to dealing with the matrimonial home, the court will attempt to arrive at an arrangement that ensures that both of you and particularly the children have a home, whilst still rewarding you both fairly for the contributions that you have made to the marriage generally and to the acquisition of the house and other assets in particular.

This is not always possible. One spouse (usually the one who is looking after the children) may therefore come away from the marriage with more capital than seems strictly fair in relation to his or her contribution because this is the only way to ensure that he or she is able to get somewhere to live after the divorce.

Generally, if you are accustomed to owning your own house or to buying it on a mortgage, the court will try to devise an arrangement for the future that will enable both of you to continue as an owner/occupier. However, this cannot always be done and, as a last resort, the court may have to come down in favour of an arrangement that provides one of you (normally the spouse looking after the children) with a home of your own and obliges the other to rely on rented accommodation, at least for the time being.

The court usually has a number of options in relation to the house. Basically there are two main sorts of arrangement possible – those that involve a sale of the house and those that enable one of you to continue to live in the house. The following are the more common alternatives open to the court, although others will no doubt present themselves in individual cases:

— the court can order that the house should be *sold* at once and the proceeds divided between you as it thinks fair. This is really only practical when the proceeds of sale will be sufficiently large to enable both of you to obtain alternative accommodation. If either of you will be able to obtain a mortgage to assist in such a purchase, the court can take this into account. However this will not always be possible, particularly for a wife who is entirely dependent on mainte-nance. The court may therefore have to consider giving a larger share to the spouse who cannot obtain a mortgage so that he or she can buy a place outright, whilst the other spouse receives sufficient to make a deposit on a property to buy with a mortgage. The one thing the court will not want to do is to order a sale of your house which will give you both some capital but to neither of you enough to buy another property – with the result that you will both have to find rented accom-modation.

— the court can order that the house should be sold *but postpone the sale* to some time in the future. This used to be done quite frequently where one spouse was looking after the children and needed to go on living in the house to provide them with a home. The court used to postpone the sale until the youngest child reached 17 or 18. Nowadays this type of order is looked upon less favourably by the courts because it is artificial to treat family life as ending when the children reach 17 or 18 – many children live with their parents, at least in holidays from college or university, for some time after their 17th or 18th birthdays. However, it may still be the only solution in some cases.

— the court can order that the house be allocated to one of you but give the other the *right to part of the proceeds of sale when the house is eventually sold*. This normally means that one of you has all the rights of an owner over the house and can decide when and if to sell it, but the other is deprived of both his home and capital asset at least for the time being. Before it makes an order of this kind therefore, the court will want to make sure that whoever does not have the house can get somewhere else to live. Sometimes this presents no real problem because he has already found a new home (perhaps because he has remarried and moved in to live with a new partner, or because he has the benefit of accommodation that comes with a job, or because he has already made arrangements to buy another property). In other cases, the court will try to make the arrangement fair by giving the spouse who does not get the home the lion's share of the family's other assets which he can use to make a deposit on a new house.

— the court can allocate the house to one of you and order that spouse to pay the other a *lump sum* forthwith in compensation. Whether this is feasible will depend on how much the spouse with the house can raise (a loan or mortgage may present insuperable problems for a spouse dependent on maintenance) and how much, if anything, the other spouse needs to purchase alternative accommodation.

— the court can allocate the house to one spouse and *compensate* the other spouse by, for example, relieving him or her of the obligation to pay any maintenance for the spouse who receives the house.

(ii) *Rented homes:*
If you rent your home from the council or from a private landlord, the court can generally allocate the tenancy to one of you, irrespective of whose name it is in. It would be most likely to do this in favour of the spouse who has care of the children.

b) THE CONTENTS OF THE HOUSE AND OTHER ASSETS
You will find the court reluctant to get involved in disputes between you over routine items of furniture and furnishings. You will be expected to decide between you what should happen to each item. People often find it convenient for the spouse who is to go on living in the matrimonial home to take the contents of the house, whilst the other spouse can be compensated by receiving other assets such as the car or a caravan. Each spouse will normally be entitled to his or her personal belongings, for instance, clothes, jewellery, etc., and to things given to him or her personally.

If you fail to agree and you ask the court to sort things out for you, you may well find that it simply orders that the whole lot be sold and the proceeds divided between you. You will both be the losers in this event as the property will inevitably fetch far less than it is worth to you or than it would cost to replace.

c) VALUABLE ASSETS SUCH AS SAVINGS, ANTIQUES, STOCKS AND SHARES

What becomes of assets such as these will often depend on the arrangement made in relation to the house. They may be required to even out the distribution of capital between you. If not, the court will divide them in whatever way seems fair, bearing in mind your needs and the way in which the assets were originally acquired. For example, a valuable antique inherited from the husband's family might be allocated to the husband and an oil painting owned by the wife before the marriage to her, whilst savings accumulated by them jointly during the marriage might be shared equally between them.

d) BUSINESS

If one of you owns a business that is, strictly speaking, property that the court can reallocate between you on divorce. In practice, the court is unlikely to make any order that will damage your business interests or force you to sell up. Nor will you be required to take your spouse into partnership with you.

However, if your spouse has helped you to build up your business (for example, by serving in your shop, or by doing the books, or helping in your hotel, or simply by staying at home and looking after domestic arrangements so that you are free to get on with your work) he or she will be entitled to have the value of this help reflected in the share he or she gets in the other family assets.

e) PENSIONS

Often one spouse has made much better pension provision than the other during the marriage and the court has to do what it can to even things up between them. For example, the wife may have devoted years of her life to looking after the children and house and consequently she will have had either no earnings or lower earnings than her husband. She may not have a pension of her own at all, having expected to share in the benefits of her husband's in retirement; or she may have a much smaller pension. (The same principles apply if it is the wife who was the greater earner and who put more savings into her pension, and the roles are reversed.)

In the type of case described above, there are various ways in which the court can compensate the wife for the benefit she will be losing in respect of her husband's pension because of the divorce. It can give the wife a lump sum from the family assets to offset the loss of her interest in the husband's pension. At one time this was the only option the courts had and it is still the preferred option in most cases if there are sufficient assets because it allows a clean break between the parties and avoids the need for costly and complicated pension valuations.

Since the Pensions Act 1995 came into effect, the court has had another option: it can 'earmark' part of the husband's pension for the ex-wife. In other words, it can order that *once the pension in question becomes payable*, the trustees or managers of the pension scheme must pay part of the pension and/or lump sum available under the scheme to the ex-wife.

Since 2000, the courts have had a further option known as pension sharing or pension splitting. It can now split the husband's pension *on divorce* and give part of it to the wife: she can keep her part in the same scheme or choose another scheme.

f) SPOUSAL MAINTENANCE

Both husbands and wives are entitled to apply for maintenance. However, the majority of claims are made by wives and this section is therefore expressed in terms of a wife's claim to maintenance. The same principles apply to a husband's claim.

The courts are obliged to consider whether it would be appropriate to make an order which would enable a couple to achieve a clean break from each other whenever possible after

divorce. Clean breaks apply only in respect of spousal maintenance, not maintenance for children. Parents have an ongoing
responsibility to maintain children, and generally levels of
maintenance are set by the Child Support Agency (see Part III
of this chapter).

If ongoing maintenance has to be paid from one spouse to
the other, a clean break will not be possible. The court is
therefore likely to investigate the possibility of an arrangement
that does not involve maintenance such as giving the wife a
rather larger than average share of the family's capital assets
so that she can be self-supporting.

Alternatively, the court may consider ordering maintenance
payments for a fixed period only (say, two or three years)
during which the wife can adjust to the cessation of her
financial dependence on the husband. Typically this type of
order might be used where a wife has not been working for a
while because she has been looking after children full time,
but she plans to go back to work in a few years' time or after a
period of retraining. Where the court makes this type of order,
it can either dismiss the wife's claims or leave them open at
the end of the fixed period. If the claims are left open, the wife
may be able to return to court at the end of the period for a
further order for maintenance if unforeseen circumstances
have arisen affecting her ability to work.

In some cases, however, a clean break is not appropriate.
For example, the court would not expect a mature wife to go
looking for employment after a long marriage during which
she has not worked outside the home. In those circumstances,
ongoing maintenance may be appropriate. If the maintenance
is ordered to last for the joint lives of the parties it will
continue until either party dies, or the ex-wife remarries, or a
further order of the court terminates or varies the order.

When deciding whether an order for maintenance is appropriate and, if so, how much, the divorce courts have an
extremely wide discretion. The outdated 'one third rule'
(where the wife would receive about one third of the joint
income of the parties) has been superseded by what is often
referred to as the 'needs and resources' approach. Nowadays

the district judge considers what each of you needs and the resources available to meet those needs, and sets the amount of maintenance accordingly.

If there are children, the court will first look at the level of child support maintenance set by the CSA (or the level at which it would be set by them) to ensure that the needs of the children, and the parent with whom they live, are met. If that parent does not have enough income, the court will try to meet the shortfall with spousal maintenance from the absent parent, if this can be done without reducing him below subsistence level.

Whether or not there are children, if money is very tight and paying maintenance at a certain level would leave one spouse without enough money to live on, the court may order that spouse to pay what he reasonably can and expect the other spouse to rely on state benefits such as income support or working families' tax credit. If there is ample money, on the other hand, the district judge may be able to increase the level of maintenance for the wife so that it covers some luxuries as well as her basic needs.

A maintenance order is not final – it can be varied at a later date if circumstances warrant a change (see Chapter 23).

Normally, maintenance will be paid directly from one spouse to the other. However, the court can direct that the maintenance order should be registered in a magistrates' court. If this is done, the maintenance will be paid to the magistrates' court, which will pass the money on to the receiving spouse. If you have any problems in obtaining your maintenance, you should refer to Chapter 22 which deals with the enforcement of orders.

PART III: CHILD SUPPORT MAINTENANCE

In this section the non-resident parent is referred to as 'he' and the parent with care of the children as 'she'. This is simply because in the majority of cases the children remain living with the mother. However, all the same principles apply where it is the father who is the parent with care.

It used to be the responsibility of the courts to make

maintenance orders in relation to children of divorced or separated parents. The Child Support Act 1991 (which came into force in 1993) created the Child Support Agency (CSA), which was originally designed to deal with all cases of maintenance for children. It is still the case that those parents with care (i.e. with whom the children live) who are in receipt of income support or jobseeker's allowance automatically have to apply to the CSA to make an assessment of maintenance against the non-resident parent. However, where the family is not on these types of benefit (even if they do receive working tax credit or disability working allowance) the regulations give them a choice whether or not to use the CSA.

The alternatives to using the CSA are simply to rely on voluntary payments from the non-resident parent, or to have an agreed level of maintenance formalised into a court order (a 'consent order'). The court does not have the power to resolve a contested application for child maintenance but it can order a variation of that order – so, if you are able to agree child maintenance at first but disagreements develop later, the court can help. After a court order has been in place for a year or more, if child maintenance arrangements are unsatisfactory, the CSA can override the court order.

If you do want to (or you have to) have your child maintenance assessed by the CSA, you will need to fill in an application form, which will ask for details about your financial and personal circumstances. Once the agency receives the application form, it sends a copy to the other parent, who then has 28 days to fill in another form and return it to the CSA: if he delays, the CSA can require him to start paying maintenance at default rates: £30 per week for one child, £40 for two and £50 for three or more. On the basis of the information supplied by both parents, the CSA calculates how much maintenance is payable on an ongoing basis and notifies the parents. As a rule of thumb, under the new, simplified regulations, the non-resident parent will pay 15 per cent of his net income for one child, 20 per cent for two and 25 per cent for three or more.

If the non-resident parent fails to pay the amount settled on by the CSA, the agency will take measures to collect it (see Chapter 22). For information about varying child maintenance at a later date, see Chapter 23.

You can get advice about how the CSA works and how it will affect you from various sources: your solicitor, a Citizens' Advice Bureau or the Department for Work and Pensions. You can ring the CSA helpline or visit their website for general advice (see Chapter 26).

PART IV: PRACTICAL CONSIDERATIONS IN RELATION TO APPLYING FOR A COURT ORDER

1. Who can apply?

Either of you can apply for a financial provision or property adjustment order. Husbands and wives are treated equally and it makes no difference whether you were the petitioner or the respondent in the divorce proceedings. In an appropriate case, you can both apply for orders in your own favour. For example, a wife might apply for maintenance and her husband might apply to have some of the family assets transferred to him.

2. When can the application be made?

Applications for long term financial provision or property adjustment orders can generally be commenced as soon as divorce proceedings have been started, though not before. It is advisable to play safe and make all the claims that you think might be appropriate at an early stage.

If you do not make an application before you remarry, you will lose your right to apply for orders (see Chapter 24). Even if you do not remarry, you may not be able to obtain an order for yourself if you delay unduly after the divorce before making your application.

3. How soon will the court hear the case?

Long term questions of financial provision and property adjustment will have to wait until after decree nisi of divorce has been pronounced. Once this has been done, the court can

consider any outstanding claims to financial provision and
property adjustment orders, although long term orders that it
makes will not come into effect until decree absolute of
divorce is granted. (Note: see Chapter 19 as regards pressing
financial difficulties before this stage is reached.)

Until recently it often took months or even years before the
court could deal with applications for financial orders. However, a new procedure was introduced in 2000 which was
designed to help the courts deal with applications more
quickly and efficiently. You (and your solicitor) will be
expected to keep strictly to the timetable for hearings and meet
deadlines for the filing and exchange of documents. The
purpose of this is to try to reduce the length of time spent on
litigation, and the cost. If you fail to attend appointments or
follow deadlines without good reason, and this results in costs
being wasted, the judge might order you to pay those costs out
of your own pocket.

4. How do I apply?

With the assistance of your solicitor you must fill in a notice
of application (Form A, which is available from the court) and
send it (and two copies of it) to the court which is dealing with
your divorce. A fee is usually payable at this stage, but you
may be eligible for fee exemption. This form simply notifies
the court and your spouse that you intend to make a financial
application. You tick boxes to indicate which orders you
intend to apply for, for example a lump sum or a periodical
payments order. You do not need to include information about
your financial position at this time, although once Form A has
been filed with the court, you will be expected to collect
together all your financial information and evidence in accordance with a strict timetable (see below).

5. What happens next?

Once the court has received your application, you will be
given an appointment with a judge, who will consider
your case at what is known as 'the first appointment'. The
court will send you and your spouse a notice of the first

appointment telling you when and where this hearing will be and which documents you will need to take with you.

The first appointment will be set 12-16 weeks from the date you filed your Form A. Although you will generally be expected to keep to the prescribed timetable, if there is good reason for it, you may be able to change (adjourn) the date of the hearing if you and your spouse agree or with the court's permission.

6. What needs to be done to prepare for the first appointment?

By the time of the first appointment, it should be clear to everyone concerned what each party's financial position is. To this end you must both fill in a financial statement (Form E). This form asks for very detailed financial information and you are obliged to complete it thoroughly. There are notes to help you do this; the more you can do yourself, the less it will cost in solicitor's fees. You must then swear on oath (or affirm) that the contents of your Form E are true – you can do this for free from a member of the court staff, or before a solicitor for a fee.

No later than 35 days before the date of the first appointment, you must file your sworn Form E at court, and exchange it with the other party (you will need to agree a date to do this through your respective solicitors). Form E asks you for information about your income, capital (such as your home, car, pension and savings), outgoings and any debts; you will need to provide certain supporting documents such as bank statements, mortgage statements, policy surrender values, a valuation of your home, payslips and business accounts.

No later than 14 days before the first appointment, you must file at court and serve on the other party a statement of the matters upon which you and your spouse agree and disagree, a chronology of significant dates in your marriage, a questionnaire requesting further information (or statement saying you don't intend to use one) and Form G on which you indicate whether or not you are in a position to proceed to a financial dispute resolution (FDR) appointment.

7. Costs

At every hearing, from the first appointment to any final hearing, you and your spouse must come to court with a completed Form H, which is a statement giving an up-to-date estimate of your costs in the financial orders proceedings. If your legal costs are run up out of all proportion to the amount of money you are hoping to recover, you (and your solicitor) will be criticised.

8. What happens at the first appointment?

You and your spouse must attend the first appointment personally. If you do not, you may have to pay the other party's costs of the wasted appointment. The hearing takes place before a judge who can, depending on the amount of information available and the level of agreement between you and your spouse, do any of the following:

- postpone (adjourn) your case to allow time for further information to be collected;
- if you and your spouse agree, make a final order;
- refer your case to an FDR hearing if the case cannot be resolved at this stage;
- adjourn the case for you and your spouse to attend mediation (for more details about mediation, see Chapter 17).

9. What needs to be done to prepare for a Financial Dispute Resolution hearing?

The purpose of the FDR hearing is to help you and your spouse to resolve the case without resorting to a final hearing. With this objective in mind, *no later than seven days before* the appointment, the applicant must file at court details of all offers and proposals that have been made or received by either party so far in the case.

10. What happens at a Financial Dispute Resolution hearing?

This is an informal hearing which you must attend personally unless the court orders otherwise. The judge will help you and your spouse to resolve matters about which you have not been able to agree. If you still cannot reach agreement, the judge will fix a date for a Final Hearing.

11. What happens at a Final Hearing?

Most cases are settled through negotiation, mediation or at an FDR appointment, but if you have not managed to do this you will need to have a final hearing.

Most of the preparation for the Final Hearing will have been done in the early stages of the proceedings. You will have set out your financial details in Form E and this evidence will form the basis of the court hearing. However, you will have to file at court and serve on your spouse a statement setting out the orders that you want the court to make. If you are the applicant you must do this *no later than 14 days before* the hearing; the respondent has to file his/her statement *within seven days* of receiving yours.

The judge at the Final Hearing will not be the same one who dealt with your case at the FDR hearing: this judge will come to the case afresh. As with the FDR hearing, you will find it relatively informal. It is private and can be attended only by those people directly involved in the case, usually yourselves, your legal representatives and the district judge. You may be asked to give evidence orally to the district judge. You may also have to answer questions from your spouse's solicitor or barrister. Your solicitor will be given an opportunity to address the district judge about your case on your behalf. The district judge will then make up his mind as to what order should be made. The normal course is for him to announce his decision immediately, so you should know the outcome of the case by the time you leave the hearing. If, however, there is any delay at any stage in the proceedings and you are in urgent need of money to live on, the district judge can be asked to make a temporary maintenance order known as an 'interim periodical payments order' just to tide you over until a final decision can be made.

12. Offers to settle

Some people are able to agree a complete financial settlement straight away when they separate, whereas others come to an agreement on the day of their final hearing; between these extremes, some resolve their cases through mediation, or at an FDR appointment, or simply by putting forward written proposals to each other through solicitors. Costs and time are saved by settling the case without resort to litigation: also, you avoid the need for someone else (the judge) to decide what should happen. Judges always try to be fair but the outcome will be out of your control.

21

Tax and Your Divorce

Tax is probably the last thing you want to think about when you are in the throes of separation and divorce. Nevertheless, you should not ignore it when it comes to making arrangements about your property and finances. By careful planning it is sometimes possible for both of you to save quite substantial sums in tax.

This is not a book specialising in tax and a detailed account of tax law would be out of place. There are many helpful publications available from booksellers that deal with all the principles of personal taxation. This chapter gives an outline of tax considerations that are of particular importance to the average person going through a divorce.

It is not usually necessary to consult an accountant about most of the routine questions that arise when you separate or get divorced – you will find that your solicitor will be able to give you the advice you need on the best way to arrange your own financial affairs. However, if you or your spouse have a particularly large income or if you have a great deal of valuable assets, you may find that you need to enlist the services of an accountant as well.

I. THE BASIC TAX POSITION

The examples given in this chapter are based upon the tax rates in force for the tax year 2004-2005. Tax rules are subject to change, particularly in the rates of tax and amounts of personal tax allowances. You should check on the current position before you decide what to do about your own affairs.

1. The basic tax position

WHAT TAXES ARE LIKELY TO AFFECT ME?

There are three taxes that are likely to affect most of us at some stage in our lives. They are income tax, inheritance tax and capital gains tax.

WHAT DO THESE TAXES INVOLVE?

a) *Income tax:* everyone is familiar with income tax – the tax that you pay on whatever income you receive. For most of us, our major (or only) liability to income tax is on our earnings from our employment.

b) *Inheritance tax*: this is potentially payable on the value of your money and property which passes on your death and on any money or property you have transferred within seven years before your death.

c) *Capital gains tax (CGT):* this is payable on capital gains that you make when you dispose of property during your lifetime. 'Disposing' of property includes not only selling it but also giving it away. So you may be liable for CGT even though you never receive the money that represents the gain in value that may have accrued between the time you acquired the property and the time when you give it away.

Although CGT is payable on disposals of most types of property, it is not payable when you give away money (sterling). There are also other exemptions from CGT, for example you are permitted to make modest gains each year free of CGT (presently £8,200 per annum) and you may also make tax free gains on the disposal of certain items, for example your car or your home. Further rules make capital *losses* allowable against gains before tax is charged. Advice may be sought if you are facing problems.

As an example of the way that tax operates in the case of a simple single gain, let us suppose that Tom buys an antique in 1990 for £10,000. In 2000, he sells it for £20,000. He has made a gain of £10,000 and he will have to pay CGT on the gain unless he can show that the disposal comes within the exceptions to the tax.

Even if Tom had given away the antique, tax could have been payable. Suppose that he gave it to his goddaughter Susan in 2000. He would be liable to CGT on the theoretical £10,000 gain. As for Susan, she would acquire the antique (it would be assumed) for £20,000, and if in due course she came to dispose of it herself, she would have to pay tax on any gain she made over this figure. Note that the actual figures would be more complex than those given in the example as tax is not, in fact, charged on that part of the gain which arises simply because of inflation ('the indexation allowance').

2. The tax position whilst you and your spouse are living together as man and wife

a) *Income tax*: until April 2000 there was a special tax allowance for married couples which could be set against either or both of their incomes, but this has been abolished.

b) *Inheritance tax*: this is not payable between spouses. It becomes payable on the estate only when the surviving spouse leaves the assets to, say, the children.

c) *Capital gains tax*: in order to understand how separation and divorce affect your capital gains tax position, you must get to grips with the position during your marriage. This section attempts to explain that position.

A husband and wife are taxed independently on his or her capital gains and each is entitled to his or her tax free allowance to set against them.

Whilst you are living together as husband and wife, you can make disposals of property to each other without incurring any capital gains tax. When one spouse – say the husband – disposes of property to the wife, she simply steps into his shoes as if she had originally acquired the property when he did. This means that no capital gains tax is payable at this stage. However, when the wife comes to dispose of the property at a later date to anyone other than her husband, she will usually have to pay tax on a gain that is greater than the gain on which she would have had to pay tax if capital gains tax had been paid at the earlier stage on the gain that had accrued so far.

To return to Tom, let us suppose that he gave the antique which he bought for £10,000 to his wife, Cheryl, in 2000 when it was worth £20,000. Neither Tom nor Cheryl would have to pay any tax on the gain of £10,000 that had been made so far, although this might have been taxed had they not been married. If Cheryl then sells the antique to a dealer in 2002 for £28,000 she will have to pay tax as if she had originally acquired the antique back in 1990 when Tom actually bought it. So she will have to pay tax on a gain of £18,000 (the original purchase price of £10,000 deducted from the selling price of £28,000) whereas if she and Tom were not husband and wife and the capital gains tax had been paid in 2000 on the £10,000 gain that had accrued so far, she would only have to pay tax for the £8,000 gain that had been made between 2000 and 2002, less indexation allowance and her capital gains tax allowance.

3. The tax position if you start to live apart
WHAT COUNTS AS LIVING APART?

You are living apart for tax purposes if:

a) you are separated under a court order or a deed of separation; or

b) you are separated in such circumstances that your separation is likely to be permanent.

HOW WILL LIVING APART AFFECT MY TAX POSITION?

a) *Income tax*: no change.

b) *Inheritance tax*: the exemption from inheritance tax which applies between spouses continues until decree absolute of divorce.

c) *Capital gains tax*: separated spouses are treated as single people for capital gains tax, save that up to the end of the tax year in which the separation takes place each spouse can continue to make disposals of property to the other spouse without incurring any CGT liability. After the end of the year of separation, you can, in theory, be liable to CGT if you dispose of property to your spouse (or ex-spouse) and make a gain. Many of the rearrangements that you have to make with regard to your property as a result of your separation and divorce may, however, be covered by the various exemptions from the tax.

4. Tax on and after the divorce
WHAT COUNTS AS A DIVORCE FOR TAX PURPOSES?

A divorce is only of consequence from the tax point of view once decree nisi has been made absolute.

WILL DIVORCE CHANGE MY TAX POSITION FURTHER?

a) *Income tax*: no change.

b) *Inheritance tax*: exemption from inheritance tax ceases once you are no longer a married couple – in other words once decree nisi has been made absolute. In the unlikely event that you wanted to leave assets to your ex-spouse in your will, he or she would have to pay inheritance tax on assets worth more than £263,000 in the usual way.

c) *Capital gains tax*: the major changes in capital gains tax arising from the breakdown of your marriage occur when you separate rather than as a result of the divorce. Once the divorce comes through, you will not be treated as a couple for CGT even if you continue living together for some reason.

WILL EITHER OF US HAVE TO PAY ANY CAPITAL GAINS TAX AS A RESULT OF SHARING OUT OUR PROPERTY ON SEPARATION OR DIVORCE?

Separation or divorce will normally involve some redistribution of your family's assets, for example, you may take the car that is partly owned by your wife and she might keep all the furniture that you have acquired jointly over the years, or you may be ordered by the court to transfer the house from your own name into your wife's name.

Until you separate (and in the year of your separation) you can make whatever reallocation of assets between the two of you that you like without any immediate liability to CGT (see page 167).

After you separate and the year is up, gains that you make on transferring property to your spouse could be chargeable to CGT depending on the type of property involved. Remember however that you will not be liable for CGT if you give away cash (for example if you make a lump sum payment to your ex-spouse after your divorce). This means that you can divide up your savings between you without any fears about CGT although, if you have to sell an item to raise money for your spouse, do not forget to take account of the fact that there may be CGT to pay immediately on any gain you make on the sale.

When you dispose of your house to your spouse (or former

spouse) it is often possible to escape entirely from CGT. This is because any gain which one makes when disposing of a property that was one's main home is exempt from CGT provided that one has not been absent from it for more than three years. Even if you have moved out more than three years ago, you may still escape CGT if you transfer an interest in the house to your spouse as part of a financial settlement on divorce or separation, provided your spouse has continued to occupy the house as her only or main residence and you have not elected to have any other property treated as your main residence.

22

Enforcing Agreements
and Court Orders Dealing with
Property and Finances

What do you do if your husband or wife tries to shirk his or
her responsibilities towards you under an agreement you have
made or under an order of the court? When problems do arise,
they are generally over maintenance. One spouse fails to pay
what he has agreed to pay or been ordered to pay by the court,
or, if he does pay, his payments are sporadic or always late or
rarely for the full amount. It is with this type of difficulty that
this chapter deals.

Problems do sometimes arise over arrangements in respect
of property. For example, the court orders the husband to
transfer the house to his wife and he refuses to do so. The
courts have machinery for ensuring that agreements made
between spouses and its own orders are complied with. A
special application to the court is required and your solicitor
will advise and help you should you find yourself in difficulties of this kind. Just to give you an example of the sort of
thing the court can do, to cope with the problem of the
husband who refuses to transfer the house to his wife, the
court could arrange for the house to be transferred without his
consent.

In this chapter it is assumed for the sake of simplicity that
the payer of maintenance is the husband/father and is thus
referred to as 'he' but the principles apply equally to wives/
mothers if they are paying maintenance.

1. Enforcing agreements about maintenance
You may have come to a formal agreement with your spouse
about maintenance (see Chapter 16). If your spouse then fails
to pay as he promised, you can take him to court for breaking
the agreement. The court can then order him to pay you

damages amounting to the arrears that have accumulated under the maintenance agreement. Each time fresh arrears accumulate, you will have to take your spouse back to court.

It may actually be easier to make a new application for maintenance through the courts – the threat of this happening may well be enough of an incentive for most people to keep to the arrangements they have agreed together.

2. Enforcing maintenance orders made by the court

In many cases, the court will make a maintenance order in favour of one spouse on divorce. If your spouse then fails to pay in accordance with the order, you can take steps to enforce it. The exact method of enforcing the order will depend on whether it has been registered in the magistrates' court.

a) *If the order has been registered in the magistrates' court*
If your solicitor foresaw any problems with your maintenance, he may well have asked for permission to register the divorce court's maintenance order with the Family Proceedings Panel (FPP) in the magistrates' court. This means that your spouse makes the maintenance payments under the court order to the magistrates' court office. They keep a record of what he has paid and pass the money on to you. If your spouse fails to pay, it is up to the magistrates' clerk at your request to chase him up and, if necessary, bring him back to court (this time in front of the magistrates) so that the situation can be remedied. The procedure is straightforward and much less time-consuming than returning to the county court to enforce a maintenance order.

There are a number of ways in which the magistrates can deal with the situation. For example:

(i) they can decide that your spouse should be excused from some or all of the arrears that have accumulated. They will then 'remit' or wipe out the appropriate amount of the arrears. Your spouse will, however, remain liable to pay your mainte-nance in the future, unless he asks, successfully, for the maintenance order to be reduced or terminated.

(ii) they can make arrangements for your spouse to pay off

the arrears in instalments along with your current maintenance.

(iii) they can make an attachment of earnings order. This can be particularly effective in securing your maintenance for you in the future. It is addressed to your spouse's employer and directs him to deduct the amount of your maintenance from your spouse's wages or salary before he is paid. The employer then hands the money over to the court who make the payment of the maintenance to you.

(iv) if all else fails and it can be shown that your spouse has the means to pay maintenance and has failed to do so, they can send your spouse to prison (for a maximum of six weeks).

b) *If the order is not registered in the magistrates' court*
If your order is not registered in the magistrates' court it is up to you to take your spouse back before the court that made the order in the first place if he fails to pay. The court will then be able to deal with the situation in a variety of ways, many of which are very similar to the remedies available in the magistrates' court. As *you* will have to prove that your spouse is in arrears with his payments, it is essential that you keep a clear and accurate record of the payments that he has made.

c) *If your spouse goes abroad*
What do you do if your spouse goes abroad and stops paying you the maintenance to which you are entitled? The courts of this country generally find it hard to enforce orders if the payer and his assets are no longer in the country. Therefore arrangements have been made with a large number of countries whereby maintenance orders can be transmitted abroad and enforced in the country where the payer happens to be.

You will certainly need legal help if you face this type of problem.

3. Enforcing child support maintenance
If your case has been referred to the Child Support Agency and child support maintenance has been assessed, the Agency will automatically collect the child support maintenance for

you if you are on state benefit and may do so on request in other cases.

If the children live with you, and your spouse has failed to make regular payments of child maintenance, the CSA may impose a deductions from earnings order (which is like an attachment of earnings order) on his employer which requires the employer to deduct the relevant amount at source from his earnings. Arrears of maintenance can also be collected in this way but in either case your spouse will be left with a minimum level of income to live on to ensure that his income is not reduced to below subsistence level.

If for some reason a deduction from earnings order is inappropriate or ineffective in your spouse's case, the CSA will be forced to take some other form of action.

It can also apply for the other enforcement procedures described in the previous paragraphs. The ultimate sanction for non-payment of child support maintenance, only used as a last resort, is committal to prison.

23

Varying Your Financial
Arrangements at a Later Date

As you have seen from the preceding chapters, it is possible to put your financial arrangements on a formal basis in two ways – by entering into an agreement with your spouse or by asking the court to make an order dealing with your property and finances. Whichever way you choose, there may come a time when the arrangements you originally made are no longer appropriate. The court does have power to vary your original arrangements in certain circumstances, on application by you or your spouse. There are a number of potential reasons for such an application including remarriage or cohabitation of the payer or payee, or a change in financial circumstances of either party. If the first wife remarries, her right to maintenance for herself immediately ceases, and if she begins to cohabit with another man on a fairly permanent basis, the husband may have grounds to apply for a variation of the order provided he can show that she is being supported by the other man. On the other hand, the husband's financial circumstances might change, for example, due to the loss or gain of a job.

Varying an agreement
If you want the court to vary arrangements embodied in an agreement with your spouse, you should refer to Chapter 16 for details of the circumstances in which this may be possible.

Varying a divorce court order
Maintenance orders: you are more likely to require a change in the divorce court's maintenance order (be it for maintenance pending suit or periodical payments) than in any other order it may make. The court can vary maintenance orders but you will have to make out a good case for the change you

seek. The court will take into account all the circumstances of your case, including particularly any changes that have occurred since it made the order, in deciding whether to grant a variation. If your maintenance order has been registered in the magistrates' court (see Chapter 22), your application for a variation will be heard by the magistrates. In other cases, it will be heard by the court that made the order originally. Do note, however, that if your maintenance claim was dismissed by the court after your divorce you cannot subsequently re-apply for maintenance for yourself.

Lump sum orders: if you were awarded or ordered to pay a lump sum in one instalment only, the court will not be able to alter this order at all on a subsequent application.

If the lump sum was to be paid in more than one instalment however, the court can vary the arrangements for payment.

Orders in relation to property: if the court made an order in relation to your property on your divorce (for example, it may have ordered your husband or wife to transfer the matrimonial home to you), neither of you can ask for this order to be altered at a later date. However, if the court granted you 'liberty to apply' or ordered a sale of some of your property when it made the order, you will be able to go back to the court for further assistance in actually putting the order into practice. For example, if the court ordered that one of you should sell the house within three months and divide the proceeds between you, and a buyer for the house cannot be found, it would be possible to apply to the court for advice as to how to proceed.

Orders in relation to pensions: if the court made an order 'earmarking' part or all of your pension or your spouse's pension, whether by way of a lump sum or periodical payments (see page 155), it has the power to vary that order at a later date. Because such orders only take effect once the pension in question becomes payable, this means that the court could vary the order before it ever comes into effect. However, the same does not apply to pension sharing orders. Like lump sum or property orders, these are intended to be 'once and for all'.

Appeals

Do not confuse applications for a variation of an order of the type described in this chapter with appeals against orders of the court. To obtain a *variation* of your order you do not need to show that there was anything wrong with the original order, merely that it would be right to alter it in the light of the present circumstances; your application to the court can be made, in many cases, a substantial period of time after the original order. On the other hand, you have the right to *appeal* against an order of the court (whether it is in relation to maintenance, or property, or a lump sum) if you feel that you have been unfairly treated. Your appeal will be heard by a more senior court and will succeed if you establish that the original order was wrong for some reason. You have only a limited period, often a matter of days, in which to indicate that you wish to appeal.

Varying child support maintenance

If you receive child support maintenance, or if you are the parent who pays it, you have the right to apply to the child support officer for a review if the circumstances have changed and the maintenance assessment is likely to be altered as a result.

One parent, for example, may lose or gain a job, change his or her working hours, or have a baby. There is no definition of a change in circumstances so any significant change in life-style or financial situation could be relevant.

Even if neither parent suggests it, the Child Support Agency (CSA) will automatically review the amount of child support payable every two years, on the anniversary of the assessment. Two weeks before the anniversary is due, the CSA will send both parents further forms asking about any changes in circumstances. When the forms are returned, it will re-calculate the amount of maintenance.

PART 7:
OTHER THINGS TO CONSIDER

24
Getting Married Again

You are not free to remarry until your divorce is made final by decree absolute (see Chapter 11). You will need to produce a copy of the decree absolute before you will be allowed to remarry. Whether you will be able to have the wedding ceremony in a church depends on the views of the clergyman concerned.

Remarriage can have an effect on your rights against your former spouse. In particular, you should bear in mind the following points:

1. When you remarry, you will cease to be entitled to receive any further *periodical payments* from your spouse for yourself (but not for the children – although since the introduction of the Child Support Act 1991 maintenance orders for children have been rare because the Child Support Agency deals with maintenance for children now: see Chapter 20). However, any orders that have already been made in relation to your property and capital will not be affected. Nor will you necessarily preserve your right to periodical payments by simply co-habiting with your new partner rather than getting married – although your right to periodical payments is not *automatically* wiped out, you could lose part or all of your periodical payments at least during your co-habitation particularly if the court feels that your new partner is contributing towards your living expenses.

2. If your spouse continues to pay maintenance to you after you have remarried, thinking that he is still obliged to do so, he can apply to the court for an order that the money over-paid should be returned to him by you.

3. If the spouse who is responsible for paying periodical payments remarries, this will not end his liability to make the payments to his former spouse and children. He can only have his liability reduced or extinguished if he can show that his circumstances have changed as a result of his remarriage so that it is no longer right to require him to go on paying at the previous rate. The court does not normally allow a spouse to ignore his obligations to his first family in favour of his new family, so it will usually be an uphill task for him to satisfy the court that his maintenance payments should be terminated or reduced.

4. Once you remarry, you are no longer entitled to start a claim for *property adjustment orders or for a lump sum* (for example, for a share in the former matrimonial home). However, if you have begun your claim before you remarry, you will be allowed to continue with it after remarriage. If you are thinking of remarriage, and your property has not yet been sorted out after your divorce, you should therefore check with your solicitor that the appropriate claims have been made on your behalf. If you were the petitioner in the divorce suit, you will probably find that all the claims you need were made automatically in your divorce petition. If not, your solicitor will be able to take the necessary steps to make the claims before you remarry. If you were the respondent in the divorce proceedings, your claim is unlikely to have been made automatically even though you may have mentioned something about property in your acknowledgement of service. Your solicitor may well have filed the necessary application form on your behalf already, but if he has not, he should be able to do so before you remarry.

5. If you have remarried or you have definite plans to do so by the time the court considers your property after the divorce, it can take your likely married circumstances into account in determining what share you should have of the assets of your former marriage. For example, a wife who is about to get married again to a very wealthy man will not require as much capital as a wife who is struggling to support herself on maintenance. If you are co-habiting with your new partner

(although you have not yet married), and the relationship appears permanent, the joint circumstances of you and your partner may also be relevant to the court.

6. Your rights in relation to the children will generally be completely unaffected by your remarriage. However, in the unlikely event of your remarrying or associating closely with someone who is totally unsuitable to be in contact with your children, you may find that you are faced with an application by your spouse to the court for an order that the children should live with him or for an order depriving you of contact with them. If the court thinks the application is justified, it can grant it (see Chapters 14 and 15).

7. Remember that (re-)marriage normally revokes your will automatically, so consider making a new one.

25

Modifying Your Will

No doubt, during your marriage, you have been quite content that a large part of your property (your 'estate') should go to your spouse after your death. However, when your marriage breaks down, your attitude may well change. It is therefore a good idea to review the question of who will inherit your property at an early stage, in many cases even before decree absolute of divorce comes through.

1. If you have no will

If you die without making a will, you are said to have died 'intestate'. A series of rules is then applied to determine who should inherit your estate.

If you die intestate *before* decree absolute of divorce is granted, as a general rule, all your personal belongings such as jewellery, clothes and pictures, will pass to your spouse together with the lion's share in your remaining property such as money, land, etc. (Exactly how much will depend on how much you leave and how many other surviving close relatives you have.)

If you die intestate *after* the divorce is finalised, your spouse will have no automatic right to any of your estate. (Your children would probably inherit the estate.) However, provided he or she has not remarried, he or she can make a special application to the court for a share of your estate on the basis that you should have provided for his or her maintenance after your death. If the court thinks it would have been reasonable for you to make such provision, it can order provision to be made for your spouse out of your estate.

2. If you have a will

If you die after decree *absolute* of divorce has been granted leaving a will made before you were divorced, then unless you have made it clear in your will that you intend your former spouse's position under it to be unaffected by the divorce, any gift you have made to him therein will automatically become ineffective, as will any appointment of him as your executor. On the other hand, if you die before decree absolute (even if decree *nisi* of divorce has been granted), your spouse will still be able to benefit from any gift to him in your will. It is therefore advisable to make a fresh will catering for your new circumstances to ensure that your property will pass to whom-ever you wish to inherit it. However, whatever you do, you cannot rule out absolutely the possibility that your spouse may make an application for provision out of your estate for his or her maintenance just as he or she could have done, had you died intestate.

Further Help and Information

There are numerous other books and leaflets available which may be of interest to you on divorce and related topics, and a considerable number of organisations to which you may like to turn for help and support. This chapter lists only a few suggestions.

Publications and Helplines

You will no doubt have come across relevant pamphlets and leaflets yourself. The Department for Constitutional Affairs (formerly the Lord Chancellor's Department) produces leaflets for people going through a divorce which are available at the offices of the divorce county court and direct from:

Department for Constitutional Affairs
54 Victoria Street
London SW1E 6QW
Tel: 020 7210 8500
Website: www.dca.gov.uk

or

FREEPOST
PO Box 2001
Burgess Hill
West Sussex
RH15 8BR

You can obtain leaflets about public funding (formerly known as Legal Aid) from:

Legal Services Commission (LSC)
85 Gray's Inn Road
London WC1X 8TX
Tel: 020 7759 0000
Website: www.legalservices.gov.uk

A wide range of leaflets about social security benefits and

child support maintenance is available from your local social security office which you will find listed under Jobcentre Plus, social security or jobcentre in the business numbers' section of the phone book or at your local Citizens' Advice Bureau. You can also get a lot of information from:

> **Department for Work and Pensions (DWP)**
> Public Enquiry Office
> Tel: 020 7712 2171
> Website: www.dwp.gov.uk

and

> **Tax Credits Helpline** 0845 300 3900

and

> **Child Support Agency (CSA)**
> National Helpline 08457 133133
> Website: www.csa.gov.uk

If you are interested in undertaking mediation and want to know more about it, you can contact:

> **Family Mediators' Association (FMA)**
> PO Box 5
> Bristol BS99 3WZ
> Helpline: 08082 000033
> Website: www.fmassoc.co.uk

The *Child Poverty Action Group* publishes very highly regarded handbooks and advice guides on – amongst other things – welfare benefits and tax credits, child support and how to cope with debt. You can contact them at:

> **Child Poverty Action Group**
> 94 White Lion Street
> London N1 9PF
> Tel: 020 7837 7979
> Website: www.cpag.org.uk

Organisations
(National Council for) One Parent Families and *Gingerbread* exist to improve the position of lone parents and their children. *One Parent Families* publish numerous useful booklets which

are free for lone parents, for example *Maintenance through the Child Support Agency, Debt, Splitting Up: The Guide for Lone Parents on Divorce and Unmarried Relationship Breakdown*. They can be contacted at:

> **One Parent Families**
> 255 Kentish Town Road
> London NW5 2LX
> Helpline: 0800 018 5026
> Website: www.oneparentfamilies.org.uk

and

> **Gingerbread**
> 7 Sovereign Close
> Sovereign Court
> London E1W 3HW
> Advice Line: 0800 018 4318
> Website: www.gingerbread.org.uk

Relate (formerly known as the National Marriage Guidance Council) provides skilled professional help from counsellors specially trained to help when a marriage is going wrong. They will not tell you what to do – they will help you to decide what is best for you and, if you decide you have to separate, they will help you to do so as painlessly as possible. They also run workshops for couples who have already decided to divorce: 'Parents apart' focuses on helping you to continue to co-parent with your ex-spouse and 'Starting again' will help you to examine the reasons for the breakdown of your marriage, and move on. They publish various titles about relationship issues including *Relate: Starting Again* by S. Litvinoff and *The Relate Guide to Step Families* by S. Hayman. You can contact them to find out where your local centre is at:

> **Relate**
> Herbert Gray College
> Little Church Street
> Rugby
> Warwickshire CV21 3AP
> Tel: 0845 456 1310

Website: www.relate.org.uk

You may also be interested in meeting other people who have had similar experiences and problems associated with divorce, through:

National Council for the Divorced and Separated
Tel: 07041 478120
Website: www.ncds.org.uk

The Samaritans, should you feel suicidal through the break-down of your marriage, will always welcome your call – day or night. Their national helpline is 08457 909090, and you will find the number of your local branch in Yellow Pages under 'Counselling'.

If you have a complaint or enquiry about your solicitor, you can contact the Law Society's Consumer Complaints Service (formerly known as the Office for the Supervision of Solicitors) at:

Consumer Complaints Service
The Law Society
Victoria Court
8 Dormer Place
Leamington Spa
Warwickshire CV32 5AE
Helpline: 0845 6086565
Website: www.lawsociety.org.uk

Further reading
There are also many good books that you may find helpful in getting you and your children through the emotional aspects of separation and divorce. Examples are *How to Cope with Splitting Up* by V. Peiffer and *Helping Children Cope with Divorce* by R. Wells. You will find these and many other books on the subject in the self-help or divorce sections of good bookshops.

One Parent Families publish a booklet called *Families Just Like Us* which contains a book list for children, from toddlers to teenagers, reflecting the full range of family lives – single mothers and their children, single fathers and their children, step families, etc. Some of the books deal specifically with the issue of divorce in a way which is accessible to children, for example, *Two of Everything* by B. Cole (for 5-8 year olds), *The Suitcase Kid* by J. Wilson (for 8-11 year olds), *Sophie* by R. Ruston (for 11+ years) and *It's Not the End of the World* by J. Blume (for teenagers). You will find many other such books in the relevant age-group sections of a good bookshop.

Index

Also in the Right Way series

GETTING THE BUILDERS IN

Everyone's heard the horror stories. Rogue contractors. Shoddy workmanship. Ballooning costs. Endless delays. Excuses and prevarication.

Paul Grimaldi's book can put an end to that. It is a clear, comprehensive guide to employing a contractor. It covers conversions/extensions, double glazing, fitted kitchens and other household projects.

FIRST TIME BUYER: FIRST TIME SELLER

Paul Jager shows how to navigate the property maze like an expert so that you can find your perfect home, successfully negotiate the purchase, organise the mortgage and solicitor, and confidently resolve common problems.

WHEN SOMEONE DIES

Estelle Catlett guides you through all the steps you need to take when a member of the family or a close friend dies: registering the death, notifying other family, friends and interested parties, organising the funeral, dealing with the will and any property that's left behind.

RIGHT WAY
PUBLISHING POLICY

HOW WE SELECT TITLES

RIGHT WAY consider carefully every deserving manuscript. Where an author is an authority on his subject but an inexperienced writer, we provide first-class editorial help. The standards we set make sure that every **RIGHT WAY** book is practical, easy to understand, concise, informative and delightful to read. Our specialist artists are skilled at creating simple illustrations which augment the text wherever necessary.

CONSISTENT QUALITY

At every reprint our books are updated where appropriate, giving our authors the opportunity to include new information.

FAST DELIVERY

We sell **RIGHT WAY** books to the best bookshops throughout the world. It may be that your bookseller has run out of stock of a particular title. If so, he can order more from us at any time – we have a fine reputation for "same day" despatch, and we supply any order, however small (even a single copy), to any bookseller who has an account with us. We prefer you to buy from your bookseller as this reminds him of the strong underlying public demand for **RIGHT WAY** books. However, you can order direct from us by post or by phone with a credit card.

FREE

If you would like an up-to-date list of all **RIGHT WAY** titles currently available, please send a stamped self-addressed envelope to

ELLIOT RIGHT WAY BOOKS, BRIGHTON ROAD, LOWER KINGSWOOD, TADWORTH, SURREY, KT20 6TD, U.K. or visit our website at www.right-way.co.uk